HOW TO PLANT AND GROW
Annuals & Perennials

Ann Reilly & Maggie Oster

©MCMXCI, Quintet Publishing Limited

This book is published by:
Modus Vivendi Publishing Inc.
2565 Broadway, Suite 161
New York, New York 10025

Legal deposit: 1st trimester 2000
National Library of Canada

Canadian Cataloguing in Publication Data
Oster, Maggie
         How to plant and grow annuals and perennials
Includes index.
ISBN 2-921556-87-1
1. Ornamental horticulture. 2. Annuals (Plants). 3. Perennials.
I. Reilly, Ann. II. Title.
SB404.9.O87   2000   635.9   C99-941456-9

Printed in Singapore.

CONTENTS

ANNUALS

PERENNIALS

HOW TO PLANT AND GROW
Annuals

Ann Reilly

INTRODUCTION

BELOW LEFT: *Tuberous begonias and lobelia combine to make a bright and bold edging and accent to this shrub planting and low rock wall.*

BELOW RIGHT: *Several different varieties of golden marigolds, backed up by a small planting of orange zinnias, bring warmth to this seating alcove set in the midst of large trees.*

BOTTOM: *Planter boxes topped with tuberous begonias reflect the cheeriness of the beds of impatiens found in this shaded backyard porch and garden.*

WHATEVER LOOK YOU WISH to have in your garden can be achieved with annuals. No matter what the weather, location, or length of the growing season in your area, you will find a wide choice within the vast range of annuals to beautify your garden. From earliest spring, when pansies' faces pop from flower beds, through the warmer summer months, when marigolds and zinnias blaze with color, into the crisp days of fall, when ornamental kale adds new tones to fallen leaves, there are annuals to fit the bill.

Annuals can be used to define areas or to accent them, to unite large sections of the garden, or to make the garden seem bigger or smaller. The tiniest of backyard gardens or balconies high over city streets benefit from containers of colorful flowers. Cut flowers can cheer up the indoors for many months. One of the nicest things about annuals is that you can change the mood they create as often as you change your mind. Go hot one year with beds of red, yellow, and orange flowers, and be cool the following year with shades of pastels, blue, violet, white, and gray.

FACING PAGE, TOP: *The need to fence in the area around the swimming pool is turned into an asset with an attractive white fence, spotted containers of tropical plants, and a low hedge of bright pink wax begonias.*

FACING PAGE, BELOW: *A massed planting of zinnias dotted with celosia is an excellent source of cut flowers and brings life to the wall in front of which it is planted.*

ABOVE: *This planting bed of tender annuals, including marigolds, zinnias, petunias, and wax begonias, is planted after all danger of frost has passed in the spring.*

BELOW: *One of the best assets of annuals is their diversity. Here, lobelia, geraniums, and zinnias combine to make a small but very attractive container garden.*

DEFINING AN ANNUAL

Technically, an annual is a plant that grows, flowers, sets seed, and dies in one growing season. Some tender perennials and biennials that will not survive cold winters but will grow and bloom in one growing season are also referred to and grown as annuals.

Annuals are divided into three categories. Tender annuals are injured by frost and are not planted until all danger of it has passed in spring, growing all summer until killed by the first frost of fall. Half-hardy annuals, although they do not tolerate frost, will grow well during cool spring or fall weather, which tender annuals will not. Hardy annuals will withstand some frost and are planted either in late fall or early spring for early color.

BELOW: *A hedge of verbena lines a garden path and leads the visitor through the arbor into the garden beyond.*

DESIGNING WITH ANNUALS

ABOVE: *A border of cineraria mixes the cool shades of violet with the warm tones of red, and adds depth and interest to the planting along this walkway.*

WHEN INCORPORATING ANNUALS into the overall design of your garden there are a number of factors you will want to consider: the size and shape of planting beds or borders; locating them to their best advantage; using them with other plants; and choosing plants because of their size, shape, and flower and foliage color.

Flower beds are plantings that are accessible and viewed from all sides. An example is an island bed in the middle of the lawn. The size of a flower bed depends on the size and scale of the property, and should take up no more than one-third of the total area in order to look in pleasing proportion to it. Beds may be formal in design, and if so are usually square, rectangular, or some other symmetrical shape with straight sides. Informal beds have curved sides and are rounded or free formed. Which you choose depends on the architecture of the house and the look you want to achieve.

BELOW: *The designer of this garden made the most of the available space by integrating a border around the pool, a border in front of the trellis, and a rim of color in the containers high in the sky.*

LEFT: *The depth of this border, which is planted with dusty miller, wax begonias, marigolds, spider flower, zinnias, snapdragons, and other annuals, is in proportion to its length.*

BELOW: *This border is designed so that it is as attractive from the outside as it is when viewed from inside the house.*

Borders are plantings at the edge of an area and are accessible from three sides at the most. They back onto the house, a wall, a fence, or a planting of shrubs or trees. To keep a border in scale and proportion to its surroundings, make it no wider than one-third its length. However, since borders can be worked from only one side, they should be no wider than five feet or it will be difficult to care for them.

The location of beds and borders depends on several factors. Select spots where you can see and enjoy them, both from inside and outside the house. Plantings at the front of the house allow passers-by and visitors to share in the enjoyment of your flowers. Look at existing, permanent features such as the house, trees, driveways, and walkways, and boundary lines between you and your neighbors and work the beds and borders into them so they complement each other best.

Your imagination is the only limiting factor. Plant annuals along garden paths; in front of fences and walls; along the patio, porch, or deck; next to garden benches; around the base of trees; under shrubs; at the base of an outside light. They can be used to attract the eye to a focal point in the garden, or to camouflage eyesores. If you're new to gardening, start small; you can always add to your plantings in following years if you find you have the time to maintain a larger garden.

ABOVE: *Moss rose is a sprawling plant that can be used to good effect in hanging containers as well as for ground cover. This variety is* Portulaca grandiflora *'Afternoon Delight'.*

RIGHT: *The dramatic foliage of coleus comes in many varieties. This plant thrives in containers, making it an ideal way to decorate a patio.*

Think about using annuals for special effects. Flowering vines are without equal as temporary screens on fences, walls, trellises, or arbors. They can be used for privacy or to block out unsightly views such as work areas and refuse storage areas. In newly planted landscapes low-growing annuals can be used as temporary quick covers while the permanent shrubs and ground covers mature.

Patios are especially comfortable when lined with borders of annuals. To increase their livability even more, set containers of annuals in the corners, next to the lounge chairs or along the steps into the house. When the containers are planted with fragrant flowers, life on the patio will be even more enjoyable. Annuals in hanging baskets can brighten dull walls and create colorful focal points.

You can plant a special cutting garden or, if space does not allow, use annuals whose blooms make good cut flowers in beds and borders so you will have bouquets to brighten the inside as well as the outside of the house.

Annuals can be used in gardens to create geometric designs or spell out your name. Before planting, lay

TOP: *Lunch on the patio is made much more enjoyable when set amidst containers of colorful annuals.*

CENTER: *An otherwise stark, modern landscape is enlivened with containers of bright red geraniums.*

BELOW: *The shaded corner of a patio is accented with a large tub of coleus.*

out the design on the ground. Select annuals with contrasting foliage or flower color so the design will stand out, and use annuals whose growth habit is compact so the design will remain intact throughout the season. Good choices for annuals to use in such designs are begonias, marigolds, alternanthera, sweet alyssum, phlox, and salvia.

The next step in creating the garden is to decide which annuals to plant. First make a list of which ones are suitable for your area by matching the plants' cultural requirements with your climatic conditions of light, temperature, soil condition, and water availability. Then decide which of these you want to grow. You can narrow down the list by keeping in mind how plant height, plant shape, type of foliage, and flower colors will fit into your garden design. You may also want to think about other considerations such as having flowers for cutting, drying, or fragrance.

Whether you plant beds and borders with one type of plant or a mixture of plants depends on several factors. Small beds or narrow borders usually look best with low-growing plants of the same type, as do formal beds. In larger plantings, a variety of heights is more interesting. The tallest plants should be at the back of the border or the center of the bed, scaling down to

TOP LEFT: *A monotonous white wall is enlivened and accented with planter boxes and hanging baskets of geraniums.*

BELOW LEFT: *The compact growth habit and extreme floriferousness of ageratum and wax begonias make them perfect choices for creating geometric designs with annuals.*

RIGHT: *Here, French marigold and ageratum are used to create distinct patterns of color.*

FACING PAGE, TOP: *A border of zinnias and marigolds fits the environmental needs of a garden that is hot and sunny.*

FACING PAGE, BELOW LEFT: *This container planting mixes the red and pink tones of dahlias, geraniums, and verbena.*

FACING PAGE, BELOW RIGHT: *Multicolored, ground-hugging portulaca makes a pretty carpet and is in striking contrast to the larger, spiked plants growing out from it.*

RIGHT: *This massed planting of bicolored red and white impatiens is an excellent example of the visual impact of planting a large area with the same variety of annual.*

BELOW: *White can be used effectively in any design, such as found in this planting of vinca, to contrast with bright colors and make them stand out even more.*

low-growing plants at the front or the edges. Against a tall hedge or fence, plant tall annuals, working down to ground-hugging plants in the front.

Plants come basically in three shapes: spiked, rounded and prostrate. A combination of all three shapes within a mixed border or bed is most attractive. This same combination of plant forms is also effective in containers and window boxes, too.

COLOR CHOICE

Color is a most critical aspect of flower-bed design. It reflects your personality and the personality of your home. A warm scheme made up of red, orange, gold, and yellow tones is exciting, happy and cheerful. It draws the eye to the garden and makes it look smaller than it really is. It also makes a garden appear to be warmer than it is. A cool scheme, which is comprised of green, blue, violet, and purple, is cooling, soothing, and calming. It makes a small garden look larger and is good when used to hide an eyesore since it does not draw attention to itself. It is also the best choice for a quiet garden designed for reading or relaxing.

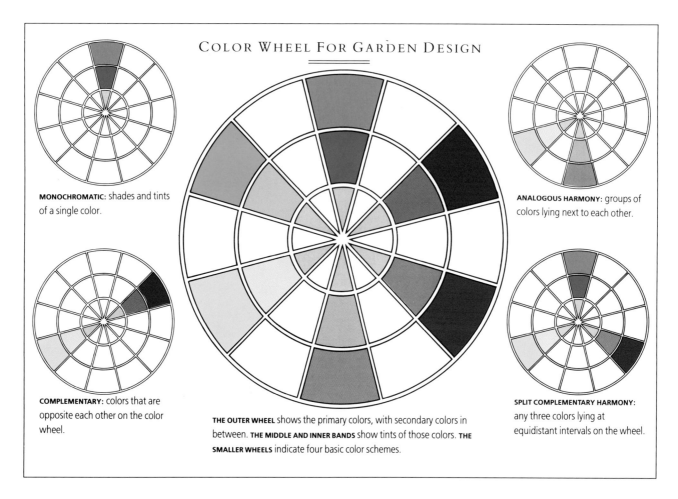

COLOR WHEEL FOR GARDEN DESIGN

MONOCHROMATIC: shades and tints of a single color.

ANALOGOUS HARMONY: groups of colors lying next to each other.

COMPLEMENTARY: colors that are opposite each other on the color wheel.

THE OUTER WHEEL shows the primary colors, with secondary colors in between. **THE MIDDLE AND INNER BANDS** show tints of those colors. **THE SMALLER WHEELS** indicate four basic color schemes.

SPLIT COMPLEMENTARY HARMONY: any three colors lying at equidistant intervals on the wheel.

To help you think more clearly about how colors work with each other you may want to buy a color wheel at an art supply store. Those colors that are across the wheel from each other, such as purple and yellow, are complementary colors. These two together create a strong harmony which may be too overpowering for a small garden but could be very striking in a larger space. In split complementary harmony, a color is used with one of the colors that is on either side of its opposite. In this case you would use yellow with either blue or red. Analagous harmony is a combination that uses three colors in a row on the wheel, such as yellow, gold, and orange, or tones of blues and violets.

It is best to start with one color as the predominant color and use one or at the most two different colors with it. Once you gain experience, you will know if you can add more colors without creating a distracting look.

Monochromatic harmony is a color scheme that uses only different shades and tones of one color. To avoid monotony in a monochromatic scheme, introduce dif-

LEFT: *Planting these impatiens in large drifts of color leads the eye down the garden path and creates a better visual effect than mixing the colors together would have. The lighter colors will also stand out at night.*

BELOW: *White candytuft, vinca, and flowering tobacco combine into an attractive planting bed using monochromatic harmony.*

LEFT: *Purple petunias planted alongside bright golden marigolds is an example of a annual planting using complementary harmony.*

ferent shapes and textures by using different types of plants, such as yellow marigolds, yellow zinnias, and yellow gazanias. You could also choose one type and one color of plant, such as pink impatiens, but plant varieties with differing shades of pink.

Pink is an excellent color for a garden that will often be viewed at night, as is white, for light colors look bright at night while dark colors fade into the background after sunset. Pastels in the night garden also add visibility to garden paths. Dark, vivid colors, on the other hand, are best in a garden that will most often be enjoyed in bright sun, for strong sunlight tends to make light colors look washed out and faded.

White can be used on its own or as a buffer or unifying color in the garden. If you use only one white plant here and another one there, you will end up with a spotty look, so use masses of white between the colors or as a unifying border in front of them. Annuals with

white, silver, or gray leaves are used in the same way as annuals that have white flowers.

Before making a final color selection, consider the color of the house, fence, or wall that the bed or border might be seen against and make sure the colors are complementary.

OTHER FACTORS TO REMEMBER

Think beyond flower color and plant shape when deciding on your list of annuals. Look also for a variety of foliage textures and colors. Some annuals have large, coarse foliage while others have finely cut leaves; a mixture of foliage types is most effective. Most annuals have green leaves, but some have leaves of red, bronze, purple, silver, or gray, which can be very useful for accents. Foliage color, although more subtle than bloom color, should also be brought into color scheme considerations when planning a design.

Annuals do not need to stand alone, although they can. Early-blooming annuals can be combined with spring bulbs, while summer-flowering annuals can be very effective when mixed with perennials and tender bulbs. Use annuals as a border or ground cover in a rose bed, or with shrubs. Annuals can also be combined in herb and vegetable gardens to bring more color and interest to them.

Think of how much maintenance you can give to the garden. When time is limited, pick annuals that do not require pinching, are not particularly prone to insect or disease problems, or have flowers that fall

cleanly as they die, so that you need not take the time to cut off faded flowers. Those annuals requiring the least amount of maintenance are ageratum, balsam, begonias, browallia, candytuft, celosia, coleus, dianthus, dusty miller, ornamental cabbage and kale, gloriosa daisy, impatiens, kochia, lobelia, monkey flower, nasturtium, nicotiana, phlox, portulaca, salvia, spider flower, sweet alyssum, wishbone flower, and vinca. Also look for those plants designated as Easy Care in the encyclopedia section.

When choosing annual varieties, you will note that some are sold in what is known as a 'series.' For example, there are 'Super Elfin' impatiens, 'Madness' petunias, 'Boy' marigolds, and 'Sprinter' geraniums. Series contain plants of the same growth habit and size but with numerous different colors. Because of this characteristic, it is best when planting different colors of the same annual to choose plants from the same series. They will be more uniform in appearance and therefore more attractive in the garden.

FACING PAGE, TOP LEFT: *The white flowers of candytuft add a refreshing purity and really stand out in the mulched bed.*

FACING PAGE, TOP RIGHT: *The silvery foliage of dusty miller adds a note of drama to this garden, both with its color and with the lacyness of its leaves.*

FACING PAGE, BELOW: *Annuals can be combined with vegetables to bring more interest to them. Here, rosy vinca reflects the color of red cabbage.*

RIGHT: *A narrow border of impatiens colors a shrub border to extend the seasonal interest after the shrubs are no longer in bloom.*

HOW TO GROW ANNUALS

Having a beautiful annual garden that you can enjoy and be proud of is not difficult. The most important thing is to start out right; don't take shortcuts to good soil preparation. Once you have this one basic under control, turn your attention to planting out the young plants and the routine maintenance tasks of fertilizing, watering, mulching, weeding, controlling pests, and manicuring the garden. If you enjoy doing things for yourself and can make the time for it, starting your own annuals from seed or cuttings can give you a great sense of satisfaction and save you considerable money. If you do plan to start your own plants this will probably be the first thing you do for this year's garden because seeds and cuttings are usually started before the garden soil is ready for working.

GROWING PLANTS FROM SEED

Starting seeds indoors in the winter and early spring is economical, an interesting challenge and sometimes the only way to grow the specific varieties you want for your garden. Although many annual seeds can be direct-sown into the garden, starting seeds indoors gives them a head start and ensures earlier blooming.

ABOVE: *When transplanting seedlings from a flat, use a spoon or, as pictured here, a label, to assist in gently lifting the roots out of the sowing medium.*

LEFT: *Always handle a seedling by its leaves, never by its stem. A plant can grow a new leaf if one is accidentally damaged, but it will not survive if the stem is broken.*

22

RIGHT: *Transplant seedlings into individual containers as soon as they have developed at least two sets of true leaves, when they should have a good root system such as pictured here.*

You can purchase flats made from compressed peat moss or plastic, or make your own containers from milk cartons, aluminum baking pans, or recycled frozen food dishes. A container can be of any size, but should be 2½–3in (6–7.5cm) deep to allow for proper root development.

The two basic requirements for containers are that they be absolutely clean and that they have drainage holes in the bottom. If you are reusing a container, wash it well with soap and water and rinse it with a 10 per cent solution of household bleach and water. Never reuse a container made of compressed peat moss for sowing seeds because you will not be able to get it clean enough, and disease organisms may be introduced.

Large seeds and seeds of annuals that are difficult to transplant should be sown into individual containers made of plastic or compressed peat moss. The roots will be disturbed very little during transplanting. This is especially true when containers of compressed peat moss are used because the entire container can be planted; roots will grow right through the peat. Such annuals are specified in the encyclopedia section.

The sowing medium can be purchased, such as loam-based mixtures designed for starting seeds. Or you can make it yourself. A good homemade mix is two parts peat moss, one part horticultural sand, and three parts sterilized soil (either purchased, or sterilized in the oven or steamed in a pot). Never use soil right from the garden for sowing seeds indoors, for it will not drain as well as a prepared soil and may also carry insects and diseases. Most seeds are started indoors six to eight weeks before the outdoor planting date. The exceptions to this are begonia, coleus, dianthus, geranium, impatiens, lobelia, pansy, petunia, salvia, and snapdragon, which all need 10 to 12 weeks.

Most seed can be planted as is but a few germinate best when chilled first or soaked or nicked to soften the seed's coating. See the lists that follow and in the encyclopedia section for these. Place pre-moistened sowing medium into the container to within ¼in (0.6cm) of the top of the container. Seedlings are prone to a disease known as damping off. When it occurs, the seedlings suddenly topple over and die. To prevent this, use only containers washed in warm soapy water that contains a few drops of household bleach; rinse well. Use fresh sowing medium; do not reuse compost for starting seeds. Such precautions will minimize the risk of damping off. If you want to be certain your seedlings will be protected, water the medium before sowing with a solution of the fungicide benomyl or thiram and let the container drain for an hour or two before planting so it will not be too wet.

It will be easier to handle seedlings if seeds are sown in rows, but this will be difficult for small seeds, which can be scattered over the surface of the medium. Except for those seeds that require light to germinate (these

are specified in the encyclopedia section and in the lists that follow) and very fine seeds, cover the seeds with enough moistened medium so that they are just covered. Seeds that require light to germinate and very fine seeds should not be covered, but rather should be pressed into the medium with your hand or with a fine spray of water.

After the seeds are sown, place the entire container into a clear plastic bag. Put the container in good light but not full sun and give it bottom heat to increase germination.

You can use heating cables purchased at garden centers specifically for providing bottom heat, or you can place the container in a warm spot, such as on the top of the refrigerator.

Some fine seeds need darkness to germinate. Since fine seeds should not be covered with potting soil, place the container into a black plastic bag until germination occurs.

Until the seeds germinate, they should need no care.

If excessive moisture accumulates on the inside of the bag, open it and let the medium dry out slightly. After the seeds have germinated, remove the plastic bag and place the containers in a sunny window or greenhouse or under fluorescent lights or special grow lights that are turned on for 12 to 16 hours a day. Once the seedlings have developed two sets of leaves, they should be thinned out or transplanted into individual containers so their roots have enough room to grow.

During the growing period, keep the containers well watered but not soggy. Bottom watering is best as it will not dislodge young seedlings and their tiny roots. Start fertilizing weekly with a weak solution (quarter-strength) of liquid fertilizer.

About one week before the outdoor planting date, start moving the plants outside during the day, returning them indoors at night, to 'harden off' the seedlings and get them used to the outdoor environment. See the following section on planting for information on transplanting into the garden.

Many seeds may be started outdoors in the beds and borders where they are to grow; some are actually best started this way because they do not like to be transplanted. Soil should be prepared first (read the section on soil), and the seeds sown according to package directions. After sowing seeds, firm the soil around them with your fingers. Seed beds must be kept constantly moist until the seeds have germinated. Since emerging weeds can often be confused with seedlings, it is best to plant seeds in neat rows and mark them carefully. Weed the bed regularly since fast-growing weeds can rob tender young plants of light, water and nourishment. Once the seeds are growing and have developed two sets of leaves, they should be thinned to the spacing guidelines outlined in the encyclopedia section. Thinnings can be transplanted to another part of the garden or given away.

GROWING ANNUALS FROM CUTTINGS

Some annuals can be grown from stem cuttings instead of or in addition to seeds. Chief among these are impatiens, New Guinea impatiens, geraniums, ivy geraniums, and coleus. Cuttings can be taken in autumn to grow these plants indoors over the winter, or from indoor grown plants to create new plants for the outdoor garden.

To root a stem cutting, cut a piece of stem that contains at least four and preferably six to eight leaves. Remove the lower two leaves and insert the leafless section of the stem into a container with pre-moistened soilless medium. Application of rooting hormone to the bottom tip of the cutting will aid in and speed up rooting.

After the cutting is in place, place the container in a clear plastic bag and set it in a warm spot with good light but not direct sun. Test the cutting for rooting after several weeks by gently tugging on the stem. If it offers resistance, roots have formed and the plastic bag can be removed. If the stem moves freely, rooting has not yet occurred. Return the cutting to the plastic bag and try again after several weeks.

Once the cutting is rooted, it can be planted into the garden or grown indoors on a sunny window-sill.

GROWING PLANTS FROM STEM CUTTINGS

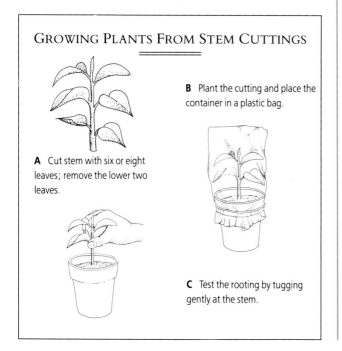

A Cut stem with six or eight leaves; remove the lower two leaves.

B Plant the cutting and place the container in a plastic bag.

C Test the rooting by tugging gently at the stem.

Seeds that need light to germinate: Ageratum, snapdragon, begonia, ornamental cabbage, browallia, ornamental pepper, coleus, calliopsis, blanket flower, gerbera, strawflower, impatiens, sweet alyssum, stock, flowering tobacco, petunia, creeping zinnia, red-flowered salvia, Mexican sunflower.

Seeds that need darkness to germinate: Calendula, vinca, bachelor's button, gazania, sweet pea, nemesia, poppy, phlox, painted tongue, nasturtium, verbena, pansy.

Seeds that require soaking or nicking before sowing: Hibiscus, morning glory, sweet pea.

Seeds that benefit from chilling before sowing: Ornamental cabbage, primrose, pansy.

Seeds that need cool temperature (55°F, 13°C) to germinate: Sweet pea, baby blue eyes, poppy, painted tongue, phlox.

Seeds that should be sown as soon as possible (they are not long-lived and should not be stored): Gerbera, kochia, salvia.

Seedlings that resent transplanting (sow seeds where they are to grow or in individual pots): Lavatera, love-in-a-mist, poppy, phlox, creeping zinnia, nasturtium.

GETTING DOWN TO BASICS

SOIL

NO MATTER HOW WELL you plan your garden or how high the quality of your plants may be, you will not succeed without a good foundation: a proper soil. Prior to planting, it is necessary to prepare the soil, especially if a flower bed has never before been in the location where planting will be done. After laying out the area, remove all grass, weeds, stones and other debris.

Incorporate organic matter such as peat moss, leaf mold, well-rotted manure, or compost at a rate of 25 to 33 per cent of soil volume into the area of the soil where the roots will be growing, which is approximately the top 8in (20cm). This means applying 2–2½in (5–6cm) of organic matter onto the soil and then digging it in to a depth of 8in (20cm).

Organic matter improves soil retention and drainage. It also improves the texture of soil, helping to make it lighter and 'fluffier,' which means there is more air in it – good for plant roots that need to breathe, and good for gardeners who find nice loamy soil easier to work. If your soil is sandy or has a lot of clay in it, more organic matter may improve its texture.

Heavy clay soil can also be improved with the addition of horticultural sand or grit. Gypsum, or calcium sulfate, can be worked into heavy soils as well. It is a good source of calcium and does not change the pH of the soil.

Flower beds and borders should not be worked in early spring when the soil is still wet or the soil texture will be ruined. Beds and borders can be worked the previous fall, or in spring just prior to planting. To test the soil to see if it is ready to be worked, take a handful of it and squeeze it. If it sticks together, it is still too wet. Wait a few days and try again. When the soil is ready to be worked, the ball of soil will crumble in your hand.

If you have sufficient organic matter, especially well-rotted manure or good compost worked into your soil each year, and if your soil pH is not too alkaline nor too acid (see the box), it should be sufficiently fertile for almost all annuals. If, however, the organic matter available to you is peat moss or leaf mold (neither of which contain many nutrients) or your soil is sandy and therefore drains quickly, washing soil nutrients away, you may need to use some fertilizer.

RIGHT: *When planting seeds directly into the ground outdoors, prepare the soil first, and rake it level before sowing.*

OPPOSITE PAGE: *Make a furrow with a rake or broom handle that is the correct planting depth for the seeds, and then sow the seeds into the furrow. After sowing, gently firm the soil back in place.*

FERTILIZERS

You have a choice between chemical fertilizers – concentrated chemical salts – and organic fertilizers – concentrated animal or vegetable sources of plant food.

Chemical types generally are available in dry and liquid form. Choose one in which the ratio of nitrogen-phosphorus-potassium (N-P-K) is 1:1:1 or 1:2:1 and apply according to label directions. The normal rate of fertilizer application on new flower beds is 1–2lb (0.5–1kg) of 5–10–5 or 10–10–10 fertilizer per 100ft² (9m²). On established beds, normally 1lb (0.5kg) per 100ft² (9m²) is recommended. Dig, rototill or otherwise mix the dry fertilizer well into the soil until it is uniform, then level the soil off with a rake. Water it in well.

Organic fertilizers are usually more expensive and slower-working, since they need to be broken down by soil microorganisms before they can be used by plants. But unlike their chemical counterparts, they will not harm valuable earthworms, and they are longer-

lasting. Calcified seaweed and seaweed extract are good all-purpose organic fertilizers for light feeding. Fish-meal, another general fertilizer, is good for using on poor soil; apply 2oz (57g) per 1yd² (1m²).

PURCHASING PLANTS

There are directions in the encyclopedia section for starting your own plants from seeds. However, you can purchase annual bedding plants instead of growing your own annuals from seed. If you buy plants, look for deep green, healthy plants that are neither too compact nor too spindly. Although it is tempting to select plants that are in bloom, it is better if they are not (except for African marigolds, which must be in bud

YOUR SOIL'S pH

SOILS for most annuals should be slightly acid to neutral with a pH of 6.0 to 7.0. A few plants like azalea, heather, and rhododendron grow best in soils that are a bit more acid (have a lower pH), but an acidic soil will not make most plants happy, and it also has a tendency to bind up certain soil nutrients, making them unavailable to plants. Earthworms, which aerate soil as they tunnel about and fertilize it with their excrement, don't like acidic soil either.

If you are not sure of the pH of your soil, test it yourself with a soil test kit; it is simple, inexpensive and can be purchased at garden centers. If the pH test results show that your soil is not within the normal range, there are some things you can do to adjust the soil's pH. For soil that is too acidic, which is more often the problem than a soil that is too alkaline, you can apply limestone. Choose ground limestone over hydrated limestone; it will not burn plants and it contains magnesium, an element beneficial for plant growth. Do not dig limestone into the soil. Spread it over the soil after it has been dug up, preferably before a rain; alternatively you can water it well. Alkaline soil is not easy to make more neutral; work lots of peat moss (which is naturally acidic) into it annually, or add sulfate of ammonia according to label directions.

or bloom when planted or they will not bloom until late summer). Most annuals will come into full bloom faster in the garden if they are not in bloom when planted.

Most annual bedding plants are grown in individual 'cell packs,' although they may be in flats or individual pots. If it's not possible for you to plant them right away, keep them in a lightly-shaded spot and be sure to water them as needed, which will probably be every day. Just prior to planting, annual bedding plants should be well watered, as should the soil in the bed or border.

PLANTING

Before you plant the annual garden, it is a good idea to lay the plan of your beds and borders out on paper. The best way to do this is with graph paper which makes it easy to draw to scale. A plan of your garden will allow you to decide the shape and size of the borders and beds in advance. In addition, you will also have a pretty good idea of how many plants you will need to

ABOVE: *When shopping for bedding plants, look for healthy, robust plants that show no signs of insects or diseases. Keep the plants in a lightly shaded spot and water them daily if you can't plant them right away.*

TOP LEFT: *This raised planting bed matches the brick paving and allows color to be introduced into an otherwise flat and uninteresting expanse.*

RAISED BEDS FOR PROBLEM SOIL

WHERE soil is poor and does not drain well, one solution to the problem is to build raised beds. Raised beds can be anywhere from about 8in (20cm) to about 3ft (1m) high and can be edged with wood, brick or stone. Because the soil is contained in the raised beds it can be improved in a much more satisfactory way than it can in the garden bed. Since the only nutrients plants will get is what you give them in their soil, be sure to use good garden soil or potting soil as you would use in other container gardening (see later). In addition to solving the problem of poor soil, raised beds are attractive garden assets and if high and wide enough their edges can double as seating areas.

TOP RIGHT: *This raised bed has been used for vegetables, but would also lend itself to annual plantings. It demonstrates one of the many forms this planting method can take.*

grow or buy. You can transfer the plan from the paper to the garden by translating the scale you've chosen (ie one square on the paper equals 1ft (30cm)) and then measuring off distances with a tape measure then laying it out with sticks and string.

Do not jump the gun on planting time! Tender annuals cannot be planted until all danger of frost has passed. Half-hardy annuals can be safely planted if nights are still cool as long as there will be no more frost. Hardy annuals can be planted in early spring as soon as the soil can be worked. Specific planting dates are outlined in the encyclopedia section.

When planting time comes, use the spacing guidelines in the encyclopedia section. Lift the plant from

the container carefully, keeping the root ball intact to avoid damage. The best way to do this is to either gently squeeze or push up the bottom of the container if it is pliable enough, or turn the container upside down and let the plant fall into your hand. If the plant does not slide out easily, tap the bottom of the container with a trowel. If the root ball is moist, as it should be, it should slip out easily without being disturbed.

Occasionally, plants are grown in containers that do not have individual cells. Separate the plants gently by hand or with a knife just prior to planting them so the roots do not dry out. Sometimes plants are grown in individual peat moss pots. To plant these, rip off a layer on the outside of the pot and put the plant and the pot into the ground. Be sure the top of the pot is below the soil level after planting or it will act as a wick and draw water away from the plant's roots.

If roots are extremely compacted, loosen them gently before planting so the plants will grow better. Dig a hole slightly larger than the root ball, set the plant in place at the same level at which it was growing, and carefully firm the soil around the roots. Water well after planting and then frequently until plants are established and new growth has started. An application of liquid fertilizer high in phosphorus is beneficial at this time to encourage root growth.

It is best to plant on a cloudy or overcast day or late in the afternoon to reduce transplanting shock. Petunias are the most notable exception to this rule, tolerating planting even on hot and sunny days.

To reduce garden maintenance, use one of the commercially available pre-emergent herbicides labelled for ornamental use. These prevent weed seeds from germinating. Such preparation will lessen your weeding chores later in the summer. Since these herbicides usually work best if they are not disturbed after application, it is advisable to apply them to the soil right after planting and water them in as required.

MAKING COMPOST

A COMPOST heap is a recycling center in your own garden. It takes leaves and other plant debris, grass clippings, fruit and vegetable scraps, and any other such matter you might have around and, with a little help from you and Mother Nature, transforms them into the best soil additive and plant food there is.

The difference between a well-decomposing pile of organic matter and a heap of rotting debris is plentiful air, warmth, moisture, and the proper balance between materials rich in nitrogen and those rich in carbon.

The pile should be at least 3ft (1m) high and 3ft (1m) wide and made up of layers of various organic matter. For example, it might start with a layer of plant debris and leaves (no diseased plants or roots of perennial weeds like bindweed or couch grass), then some grass clippings, a layer of kitchen waste (no meat or fats), then a sprinkling of soil, and then a repetition of such layers. Cover the whole with another sprinkling of soil, and water it until the pile is moist but not soggy.

Let it stand for a week and then turn the pile with a pitch fork so that all the layers get mixed up and it is aerated. Turn again every two weeks and water if necessary. If the material you added to the pile was in relatively small pieces and the temperature outdoors is warm, you should have finished compost in about three months.

To ensure a well-decomposed compost – especially if your supply of nitrogen-rich plant matter like grass clippings and green leaves is not abundant – you can add blood meal or a commercial 'compost-making enzyme' to the pile as you layer it. If you have access to animal manure, add thin layers of it between thicker layers of plant matter as you make your heap, and let the pile stand for a year before you use it in the garden to make sure the manure is fully decomposed.

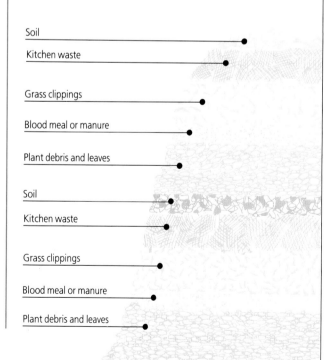

Soil

Kitchen waste

Grass clippings

Blood meal or manure

Plant debris and leaves

Soil

Kitchen waste

Grass clippings

Blood meal or manure

Plant debris and leaves

Growing the Annual Garden

The first steps to a beautiful flower garden, as we have seen, are selection of the right annuals, good soil preparation and proper planting. After that it's up to you and Mother Nature to keep the garden at its peak of color and beauty.

Fertilizing

Most annuals do not require high levels of fertilizer, but will grow and flower better if adequate nutrients are available. The notable exceptions to this are nasturtium, spider flower, portulaca, cosmos, gazania, or salpiglossis, which like to be grown in poor, infertile soil. With these, add little or no fertilizer to the soil at planting time.

For maximum growth and flowering, fertilize once or twice more during the growing season with 5–10–5 or a similar granular fertilizer at the rate of 1–2lb (0.4–1kg) per 100ft² (9m²). As an alternative, you may use a liquid fertilizer such as 20–20–20, following label directions, and apply it every four to six weeks. Over-fertilizing will cause a build up of soluble salts in the soil, especially if it is heavy soil, and result in damage to the annuals. Over-fertilizing can also result in heavy foliage growth and few flowers. If your plants are not blooming properly, don't be tempted to add more fertilizer; eliminate it completely.

Watering

Deep, infrequent watering is better than frequent, light applications of water, as the former encourages deep root growth which results in healthier plants. Most annuals need to be watered about as often as the lawn does. Refer to the individual plant descriptions in the encyclopedia section. When dry soil is called for, allow the top inch (2.5cm) of soil to become dry before re-watering. When moist soil is required, never the let the soil surface dry out. Annuals with average water requirements can be watered when the soil surface becomes dry.

If possible, do not let the foliage become wet during watering, as this can spread disease. Soaker hoses that are porous, so that water slowly leaks out onto the ground, or other methods of ground watering are the best way to achieve this. However, if overhead sprinklers must be used, you should water those annuals that are disease prone (zinnias and calendula in particular)

LEFT: *This type of irrigation system, in which water is carried to the plants through narrow tubing from the main hose, permits you to water the plants where they need it, at the roots, and therefore not waste precious water or get the foliage wet.*

RIGHT: *Some annuals are weak-stemmed and will not stand upright by themselves. Stakes such as this one correct the problem yet are still attractive.*

as early as possible in the day so that the foliage will dry out before the night. When growing annuals for cut flowers, do not water them overhead if at all possible to prevent water damage to the blooms.

Where rainfall is low and water supplies are short, choose a drought-resistant annual such as portulaca, celosia, cosmos, sunflower, candytuft, dusty miller, gazania, spider flower, sweet alyssum, or vinca.

MULCHING

After your annuals are planted, adding a 2- to 3-in (5–7.5cm) layer of mulch will not only make the garden more attractive, it will also keep weeds down and conserve soil moisture. The best mulches are organic in nature, and include bark chips, pine needles, shredded leaves, peat moss, or hulls of some kind. The following year, the mulch can be incorporated into the soil before planting, enriching it. Additional mulch can be added each spring, resulting in better soil structure and therefore better growth as years pass.

If the summers in your region are hot, annuals that require cool soil should be mulched immediately after planting, as this will keep the soil cool into the summer. Annuals that like warm soil should not be mulched until the weather and the soil has warmed up. Black plastic mulch can be used to keep the soil warm while reducing weeds. Be sure there are enough holes in the plastic for water to penetrate into the soil below.

STAKING AND TYING

Most annuals do not need to be staked, but now and then a few of them do, because they are heavy or too tall to stand up by themselves. Use a sturdy stake of wood or bamboo and tie the plant to it loosely with a twist tie or string. Don't tie too tightly or the stem will be pinched or damaged. Large bushy plants may need three or four stakes around the outside of the plant to keep them upright and compact. Large plants can also be staked with large wire cones, often called tomato cages, or with similar devices.

Some vines will cling on their own, but others need help. Tie vines loosely to their supports without tying so tight as to damage the stems. Vines can also be woven through trellises and fences made of chicken wire or similar material.

WEEDING

Weeding is more than removing unwanted plants that make flower beds and borders unattractive. Weeds compete with annuals for water, light, and nutrients, and are breeding grounds for insects and diseases. Weeds will appear, even if you use mulch. Be sure to remove them as soon as possible. Remove weeds carefully, especially when the annuals are young, so you do not disturb the annuals' roots. Weeds can be pulled by hand or, when the annuals are mature, worked out with a hoe.

SELF-SOWING

Some annuals, particularly impatiens, portulaca, salvia, and nicotiana, will self-sow, or reseed themselves, from one year to the next, or sometimes during the same growing season. The seedlings of hybrid plants will not be identical to the parent and will often be less vigorous. It is best to remove these and replant all flower beds and borders with new annuals each year for maximum effect. Seeds of non hybrid plants can be left to grow if you wish, and the annuals will act as though they were perennials. However, in areas with short growing seasons, these seedlings may never grow large enough to be showy, so you can't rely on this and will need to replant.

PINCHING AND PRUNING

A few annuals, primarily petunias, snapdragons, and pansies, may need to be pinched back after planting or after the first flush of bloom to keep them compact and freely flowering. As new and more compact hybrids are created, this is becoming less important. Sweet alyssum, candytuft, phlox, and lobelia may tend to sprawl and encroach on walks, the lawn or other flowers. They can be headed back with hedge clippers if this occurs. This shearing will also encourage heavier blooming. When flowers are taken from annuals as they fade or when cut for cut flowers, the plants are in effect being pruned.

DEAD-HEADING

Some annuals, chiefly begonias, impatiens, coleus,

alyssum, ageratum, lobelia, vinca, and salvia, require little additional care. Their flowers fall cleanly from the plant after fading and do not need to be manually removed. Others, such as marigolds, geraniums, zinnias, calendula, and dahlias, will need to have their faded flowers removed. This is known as dead-heading and is necessary to keep the plants, attractive in full bloom, from going to seed, and to prevent disease. Dead-heading can be done with pruning shears or sometimes with the fingers.

FALL CARE

In the fall, after frost has blackened the tops of annual plants, they should be removed so the beds are not unsightly through the winter. Removal of plants also eliminates sites where insects and diseases can shelter during winter. Dig or pull them out and put them on the compost pile, if the plants are not diseased or infested with insects.

ABOVE: *Tall dahlias are staked to stand upright, which creates a pretty pattern against the white wall. Always drive stakes at planting time so that the roots are not accidentally damaged later on.*

INSECT AND DISEASE CONTROL

ANNUALS CAN BE relatively trouble free, with a few insects and disease problems, provided they receive proper care. Here are the most common problems that may develop:

INSECTS

■ APHIDS

These are very small, winged insects that are light green, brown or cream in color; the light green aphids are the most common on annuals. Their presence is usually noticeable by the honeydew they exude as they suck sap. This sticky substance attracts ants and sometimes encourages a sooty mold to grow on it. A heavy infestation can stunt or deform plant growth and prevent flowers from developing properly.

If not many plants are infested, the aphids can often be washed off quite easily with a solution of soap and water. Organic sprays include derris, pyrethrum, and quassia. Diazinon, malathion, and sevin are effective chemical insecticides. Ladybugs, natural predators of aphids, should be encouraged.

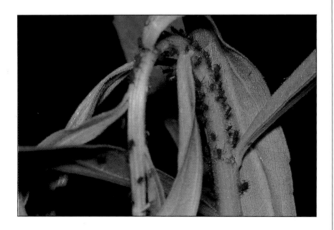

ABOVE: *Aphids are the best known cause of plant damage.*

■ MEALY BUGS

These cottony white insects can be found on the undersides of leaves and on stems. For small infestations wipe off with a damp cloth. Pull out and burn badly infested plants. Diazinon or malathion will only help if the affected areas are sprayed heavily.

■ EARWIGS

Recognizable for their large pinchers, earwigs hide inside flowers and come out to eat ragged holes in the petals and leaves. Since they like to hide, trap them in inverted flower pots under which you have placed dry leaves, straw, or crumpled newspaper. Alternatively, spray plants with diazinon, malathion or sevin.

■ SLUGS AND SNAILS

Slugs and snails eat green leaves, especially those of young plants, often weakening them so much that they die. Remove any moist or soft mulch around plants and replace with a mulch of sand or another rough, dry mulch.

Sink saucers in the soil around susceptible plants and keep filled with beer as it evaporates. Remember to replace beer that becomes diluted with rainwater; remove dead slugs that go in for a drink but can't climb out again.

■ THRIPS

These are tiny black insects that suck sap from leaves and flowers, leaving silver streaks in their paths. They can wither the edges of flowers and distort them. They are most prevalent during hot, dry weather. Spray with the organic insecticide derris, or chemical sprays and dusts like diazinon, malathion, or nicotine.

■ CATERPILLARS

Larvae from several kinds of moths and butterflies can eat buds and foliage. Insects sometimes roll themselves in leaves in spring. Spray with the organic insecticide derris, pick off the infested shoots by hand, or use a chemical spray of diazinon or sevin.

DISEASES

■ DAMPING OFF

This is any one of a number of diseases that causes a fungus to rot seedlings at the soil level; they topple over and die. Prevention is best: use a sterile sowing medium; clean all containers and tools with soap and water containing a few drops of household bleach, then

RECOGNISING COMMON INSECTS

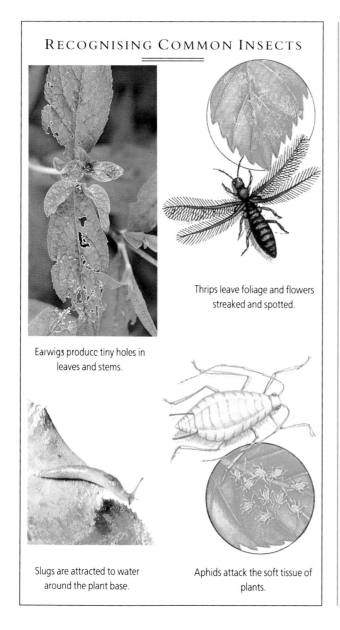

Earwigs produce tiny holes in leaves and stems.

Thrips leave foliage and flowers streaked and spotted.

Slugs are attracted to water around the plant base.

Aphids attack the soft tissue of plants.

rinse well. Don't sow seeds too thickly and be careful not to overwater. For extra protection, treat the soil before sowing with a fungicide like thiram or benomyl. Should the condition exist, you may be able to control it by watering with captan or thiram.

■ POWDERY MILDEW

Affected plants will be coated with a fine white or gray powder and they will be stunted. Prevention is best: plant those plants most susceptible to it, like chrysanthemum, delphinium, and Michaelmas daisy, in an open area not too close together; do not let the plants get too dry by mulching them and watering regularly in dry times. Remove diseased plants promptly.

■ RUST

A variety of fungi may cause yellow and green mottlings on the upper surfaces of leaves and orange or brown spots on the undersides. Plant disease-resistant cultivars of those plants most affected, like antirrhinum, chrysanthemum, hollyhock, and Sweet William. Keep plants healthy by watering and fertilizing as needed. Remove and burn infested plants.

■ VIRUS

Since there are several viruses that can affect plants, the symptoms vary, but generally affected plants are stunted with deformed, mottled leaves. Flowers may be misshapen or fail to develop. Since there is no cure or real control, prevent by buying virus-resistant cultivars and keep plants healthy. Remove and burn infested plants promptly.

COMMON PLANT DISEASES

RIGHT Examples of the damage caused by (left to right) virus, damping off and powdery mildew.

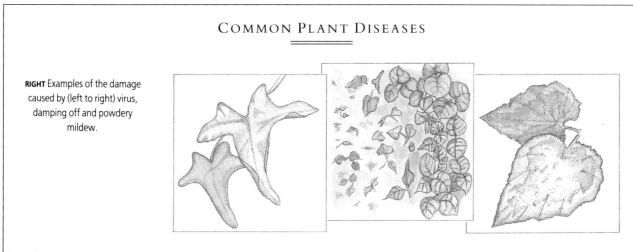

GROWING ANNUALS IN CONTAINERS

GROWING ANNUALS IN CONTAINERS requires more maintenance than caring for the same plants in the ground, but the ability to bring color into the landscape without planting beds makes it worth the effort. The container can be made of wood, stone, ceramic, plastic, or anything that will hold planting medium and plants, as long as it has adequate drainage. Metal containers may get too hot in the sun. You can use your imagination and plant container gardens in discarded tires, old shoes, bird cages, boxes, wheelbarrows, or tree stumps.

If the container does not have drainage holes and none can be made, a thick layer of small stones must be placed in the bottom of the planter to prevent water-logging of the roots.

Garden soil, if of good quality, can be used in the container so long as you lighten it up by mixing in some potting soil, peat moss, or another similar soil conditioner, so that it is not too heavy and drains prop-erly. If you have poor soil or your garden is prone to insect or disease problems use a potting soil. Fill the container to about ½in (1cm) from the top before plant-ing and water well. Space plants closer than you would space them in the ground for a fuller effect.

Containers will need to be watered more often than beds and borders, as the growing area is limited and more prone to drying out, especially if the containers are made from a porous material like clay or are kept in the sun or the wind. Daily watering may be necessary, so make sure a garden hose is accessible. Containers should also be fertilized lightly but frequently with a liquid plant food.

If light strikes the planter unevenly, the growth of the plants in the container will be uneven. Rotate the container frequently in order to avoid this problem. Large containers are easier to move if they are placed on wheels or casters.

ABOVE LEFT: *Garden geranium thrives in containers, and is well suited to hanging baskets.*

ABOVE RIGHT: *This herb garden is an easy maintenance idea, showing some of the possibilities for outdoor container plants.*

GUIDE TO PLANTS FOR SPECIAL CONDITIONS

Plants for heavy shade – Begonia, coleus, impatiens, monkey flower, wishbone flower.

Plants for partial shade – Ageratum, balsam, black-eyed Susan vine, browallia, dusty miller, forget-me-not, lobelia, nicotiana, ornamental pepper, pansy, salvia, sweet alyssum.

Plants for dry gardens – African daisy, amaranthus, celosia, dusty miller, globe amaranth, kochia, petunia, portulaca, spider flower, strawflower.

Plants for moist gardens – Balsam, painted tongue, tuberous begonia, black-eyed Susan vine, browallia, calendula, ornamental cabbage and kale, China aster, gerbera, impatiens, lobelia, monkey flower, nicotiana, ornamental pepper, pansy, phlox, stock, wishbone flower.

Plants for the seashore – Blanket flower, candytuft, nicotiana, lobelia, love-in-a-mist, marigold, Mexican sunflower, morning glory, petunia, phlox, portulaca, spider flower, sweet alyssum, vinca.

Plants for hot gardens – Amaranthus, anchusa, balsam, blanket flower, celosia, coleus, creeping zinnia, dusty miller, gazania, gloriosa daisy, globe amaranth, kochia, triploid marigold, nicotiana, ornamental pepper, petunia, portulaca, salvia, spider flower, strawflower, verbena, vinca, zinnia.

Plants for cool gardens – African daisy, painted tongue, tuberous begonia, browallia, calendula, dianthus, flowering cabbage and kale, lobelia,

Plants for alkaline soil – Aster, painted tongue, dianthus, strawflower, sweet pea.

Hardy annuals – African daisy, baby blue eyes, bachelor's button, calendula, flowering kale and cabbage, hibiscus, lavatera, pansy, phlox, snapdragon, stock, sweet alyssum, sweet pea.

Fragrant annuals – Dianthus, snapdragon, spider flower, four o'clock, stock, sweet alyssum.

Annuals for hanging baskets – Begonia, black-eyed Susan vine, browallia, coleus, creeping zinnia, impatiens, ivy geranium, lobelia, petunia, vinca.

Annuals for cut flowers – Ageratum, aster, blanket flower, calendula, cosmos, dahlia, gerbera, marigold, salvia, snapdragon, spider flower, zinnia.

NB These lists are general guides only. See the Encyclopedia section for further details of the conditions preferred by specific plant species.

ENCYCLOPEDIA SECTION

*T*hroughout this section, indications have been made when a variety has won an award, making it a plant of particular merit. These awards are All America Selections (AAS); All Britain Trials (ABT); Fleuroselect (FS) and Royal Horticultural Society (RHS).

GUIDE TO USING THE ENCYCLOPEDIA SECTION

■ Annuals are arranged alphabetically, according to Latin name.

■ Below each entry is a chart of symbols that provide easy reference to information on specific temperature, soil or positioning needs, or to plants which are recommended for certain uses.

 Easy care

 Heat tolerant

 Full shade

 Cold tolerant

 Partial shade

 Acid soil

 Full sun

 Alkaline soil

 Dry conditions

 Hanging baskets

 Moist conditions

 Cut flowers

 Seashore use

 Fragrant

Ageratum Houstonianum 'MADISON'

AGERATUM HOUSTONIANUM

AGERATUM, FLOSS FLOWER

CLUSTERS OF TINY fluffy, powderpuff-like flowers of primarily blue but sometimes pink or white cover 6–12in (15–30cm) mounded plants that have heart-shaped leaves. Use in borders, edgings, and container plantings. Good varieties include 'Blue Blazer', 'Blue Danube', ('Blue Puffs'), 'Blue Ribbon', 'Madison', 'North Sea', 'Royal Delft', 'Pink Powderpuffs', 'Summer Snow', and 'Southern Cross'.

■ **HOW TO GROW** Seeds can be sown outdoors after all danger of frost has passed, but better results are obtained by starting seeds indoors six to eight weeks earlier. Do not cover seeds as they need light to germinate which takes five to 10 days. Space plants 6–8in (15–20cm) apart in sun or light shade. Ageratum prefers rich, moist, well-drained soil and grows best under moderate heat and humidity. Ageratum flowers fall cleanly as they fade. Leggy plants can be sheared back.

ALTERNANTHERA FICOIDEA

ALTERNANTHERA, COPPERLEAF

ALTERNANTHERA IS GROWN for its ornamental foliage which is green, red with orange, yellow, yellow with red, rose, purple and copper, or blood red. It is a neat, trim plant only 6in (15cm) high. The plant is generally sheared, preventing the inconspicuous flowers from blooming. Where an intricate, formal design is called for in the landscape theme, alternanthera is one of the best plants to use.

■ **HOW TO GROW** Alternanthera is grown from divisions or cuttings as it cannot be propagated from seed. It is best to root cuttings in the late summer and overwinter them in a greenhouse or a hot bed if available, setting them into the garden in spring after danger of frost has passed. Set plants 8–10in (20–25cm) apart in a warm, sunny location and an average garden soil. Keep plants clipped, especially if they are being used in a pattern.

Alternanthera ficoidea 'BRILLIANT'

ALTHAEA ROSEA

HOLLYHOCK

MOST HOLLYHOCKS ARE stately 4–6ft (1.2–1.8m) plants, but there are dwarf varieties that grow only 24in (0.6m) high. Both have stiff spikes of paperlike flowers on top of maplelike leaves. Flowers may be single or double in a wide range of colors except blue. Some hollyhocks are perennials or biennials but can be grown as annuals. Use them as accent plants or at the back of the border.

Varieties to choose from are 'Majorette' (AAS), 'Pinafore', 'Powder Puffs', and 'Summer Carnival' (AAS).

■ **HOW TO GROW** Start seeds indoors six to eight weeks before the last frost, not covering the seeds which need light during the 10 to 14 day germination. Set plants 18–24in (46–60cm) apart in full sun or very light shade. Soil should be rich, moist and well drained. Tall hollyhocks need staking. Cut flowers as they fade; hollyhock self-sows easily but plants will be inferior. It is susceptible to rust; see Diseases, earlier.

Althaea rosea

AMARANTHUS

AMARANTHUS

All members of this plant grouping have one thing in common: bright, flashy, multicolored foliage. Leaves can be red, maroon, chocolate, green, or yellow, variegated and splashed with one or more contrasting colors. They are a colorful addition to beds, borders, hedges, and pots, and are also good accent plants. *A. caudatus*, love-lies-bleeding or tassel flower, is an upright 3–5ft (1–1.6m) plant that is topped with trailing, ropelike, bright red 2ft (0.6m) flowers. *A. tricolor*, Joseph's coat, is a 2ft (0.6m) plant with leaves that are deep green, chocolate or yellow at the bottom of the plant and bright crimson and gold at the top. *A. tricolor salicifolius*, fountain plant or summer poinsettia, grows 2–4ft (0.6–1.3m) tall. This variety is distinguished by the dark green leaves at the bottom and bright green leaves at the top.

■ **HOW TO GROW** Plant seeds outdoors after all danger of frost has passed, or for best results start seeds indoors three to four weeks earlier. Germination takes 10 to 15 days. Plant 18–24in (45–60cm) apart in average to infertile garden soil in a warm, sunny spot. Amaranthus tolerates drought and heat.

Amaranthus tricolor

Ammobium alatum 'GRANDIFLORA'

AMMOBIUM ALATUM 'GRANDIFLORA'

WINGED EVERLASTING

WINGED EVERLASTING HAS 1in (2.5cm) flowers with glistening, silvery white petals and yellow centers on 36in (90cm) stems. Leaves are soft, woolly, and silvery on thick, branching stems with raised edges or 'wings.' An interesting addition to either the cut flower garden or a dried bouquet, winged everlasting is actually a biennial or half-hardy perennial grown as an annual.

■ **HOW TO GROW** Seeds may be sown outdoors six weeks before the last frost, or started indoors six to eight weeks earlier. Germination takes five to seven days. Where winters are warm, seeds may be sown outdoors in autumn up to two months before the first autumn frost. A light covering of mulch will protect the plants from possible frost damage.

Set plants 15in (38cm) apart in full sun and sandy, rich, moist, well-drained soil.

To dry flowers, cut them before they mature and hang them upside down in a cool, dry, shady place.

SUMMER FORGET-ME-NOT, BUGLOSS

SUMMER FORGET-ME-NOT HAS clusters of tiny ultramarine flowers on showy, spreading plants that grow 9–18in (23–46cm) tall. Foliage is coarse, lance-shaped, and hairy. Use for borders, edgings or as a ground cover. Good varieties are 'Blue Angel' and 'Blue Bird'.

■ **HOW TO GROW** Sow seeds directly into the ground after all danger of frost has passed, or start plants indoors six to eight weeks earlier. Germination takes 14 to 21 days. Plant summer forget-me-not in full sun, 10–12in (25–30cm) apart. Soil should be light, infertile, dry, and well drained. Cut back after flowering to encourage a second bloom.

Anchusa azurea 'DROPMORE'

Antirrhinum majus

ANTIRRHINUM MAJUS

SNAPDRAGON

THIS PLANT GOT ITS NAME from its original form, which resembled the jaw of a dragon ready to snap. Today, these curious, sac-shaped, two-lipped flowers have been joined by open-faced and double blooms. All appear on showy, erect spikes over dark, straplike foliage. Snapdragon flowers come in all colors except true blue and have a light, spicy fragrance. Grow in borders, beds, or rock gardens, or as exquisite and long-lasting cut flowers.

Depending on the variety, plants are 6–36in (15–90cm) high. Low-growing varieties are 'Floral Carpet', 'Royal Carpet' (RHS), and 'Kolibri'. Medium-sized varieties are 'Coronette' and 'Little Darling' (AAS, ABT). Tall types are 'Bright Butterflies', 'Madame Butterfly' (AAS, ABT), and 'Rocket'.

■ **HOW TO GROW** Seeds may be sown outdoors in midspring after the soil has started to warm up, but for best results, sow indoors six to eight weeks earlier. Do not cover seeds as light is needed for germination, which takes 10 to 14 days.

Depending on their ultimate height, plant snapdragons 6–15in (15–38cm) apart in full sun or light shade. Overcrowding encourages diseases like mildew and rust; see Diseases, earlier. Pinch young plants to induce branching and produce more flowers.

Soil should be light, rich, slightly moist, and well drained. After flower spikes have faded, cut them off to encourage a second and third bloom. Although snapdragons were traditionally cool weather plants, newer hybrids are more heat resistant. In warm areas, snapdragons will overwinter as perennials.

46

ARCTOTIS STOECHADIFOLIA

AFRICAN DAISY

ODERN HYBRIDS OF THE African daisy have yellow, white, pink, bronze, red, purple, brown, and orange flowers and grow only 10–12in (25–30cm) tall. Flowers bloom all summer but close at night. Use them in beds and borders.

■ **HOW TO GROW** Seeds can be sown outdoors in early spring as soon as the soil can be worked, but for best results, start them indoors six to eight weeks before the last frost, when the seedlings should be set outside. Germination takes 21 to 35 days.

Set plants 12in (30cm) apart in full sun and in a light, dry, infertile, sandy soil. African daisies grow best where nights are cool. Remove faded blooms regularly to prolong flowering and improve appearance.

Arctotis stoechadifolia

Begonia x semperflorens-cultorum

BEGONIA X SEMPERFLORENS-CULTORUM

WAX BEGONIA, FIBROUS BEGONIA

WAX BEGONIA HAS neat mounds of round foliage and single or double flowers. The tiny blooms of white, pink, rose, or red appear continuously over waxy green, bronze, brown or variegated foliage on a plant that grows 6–12in (15–30cm) high. Plant in beds, as edgings or in containers. Varieties include 'Avalanche', 'Bingo!', the 'Cocktail' series ('Brandy', 'Gin', 'Rum', 'Vodka', 'Whiskey'), 'Coco', 'Double Ruffles', 'Foremost', 'Glamour', 'Lucia', 'Party', 'Pizzazz', 'Prelude', 'Scarletta', 'Tausendschon', 'Varsity', and 'Wings'.

■ **HOW TO GROW** Start seeds indoors 12 to 16 weeks before the last spring frost. The seeds are fine and dusty and need light during the 15- to 20-day germination period. Set plants 6–8in (15–20cm) apart in partial shade; hybrid wax begonias can be set in full sun if temperatures do not exceed 90°F (32°C). In hot areas, select bronze-leaved wax begonias over the green-leaved forms for their greater heat resistance. Soil should be very rich, fertile, well drained, and of average moisture.

BEGONIA X TUBERHYBRIDA

TUBEROUS BEGONIA

TUBEROUS BEGONIAS GROW to a height and width of 12in (30cm). Their double blooms of red, white, yellow, orange, or pink in solids and bicolors resemble tiny roses or camellias and bloom in hanging clusters. Tuberous begonias can be grown in beds or as edgings, and are magnificent in hanging baskets. Well-known varieties include 'Clips' and 'Non Stop' (FS).

■ **HOW TO GROW** Start seeds indoors 16 weeks before the last spring frost, and give them 24 hours of light during germination, which takes two to eight weeks. You can start tubers indoors eight weeks before the last frost. Plant them, round side down, in flats of peat moss and perlite set in bright light. Do not overwater. Set plants 12in (30cm) apart in part to full shade. Soil for tuberous begonias must be very rich, moist, fertile, and well drained. Tuberous begonias prefer a slightly cooler temperature than wax begonias, and benefit from high humidity or frequent misting. In the fall, tuberous begonias can be lifted from the soil and the tubers dried and stored over winter in a cool, dark, dry place.

Begonia x tuberhybrida

Brachycome iberidifolia   'PURPLE SPLENDOR'

BRACHYCOME IBERIDIFOLIA

SWAN RIVER DAISY

MASSES OF FRAGRANT, 1½in (4cm) daisylike flowers in blue, red, rose, white, or violet with dark centers smother 9–18in (23–46cm) mounded plants in summer. Under the flowers, the almost invisible foliage is featherlike. Swan River daisy is well suited for rock gardens, containers, and borders, and as a cut flower.

■ **HOW TO GROW** Start seeds indoors four to six weeks before the last frost. Germination takes 10 to 18 days. Set plants 6in (15cm) apart in full sun and rich, moist soil. Swan River daisy is not a long-blooming plant, so successive plantings should be made three weeks apart to ensure continual bloom. Swan River daisy prefers cool temperatures.

BRASSICA OLERACEA, ACEPHALA GROUP

ORNAMENTAL KALE AND CABBAGE

ORNAMENTAL (FLOWERING) KALE and cabbage have open rosettes of green leaves, with central leaves colored in white, pink, or purple. Plants measure 12–15in (30–38cm) across and 10–12in (25–30cm) high. They are a most unusual and decorative annual used primarily in the fall and winter. Varieties include 'Nagoya', 'Osaka', and 'Peacock'.

■ **HOW TO GROW** Start seeds indoors six to eight weeks before setting plants outdoors. Seeds of ornamental cabbage must be chilled for three days in the refrigerator before sowing and should not be covered as they need light to germinate. Germination of ornamental kale is not aided by either light or chilling; both germinate in 10 to 14 days.

Space plants 12–15in (30–38cm) apart in full sun and rich, moist soil. The essential factor in growing ornamental kale and cabbage is cool temperatures; plant about one month before the first expected fall frost. Coloration starts at 50°F (10°C), and is intensified by frost. Plants last all winter where the temperature does not drop below 20°F (−6.5°C).

Brassica oleracea

Browallia speciosa

BROWALLIA SPECIOSA 'MAJOR'

BROWALLIA

STEMS GROW 8–18IN (20–45CM) LONG and carry a multitude of purple, blue, or white starlike to bell-shaped, velvety, 2in (5cm) flowers. Browallia is a good bedding plant, but it really comes into its own as a container plant on patios and decks as it has trailing, cascading stems. Varieties include 'Blue Bells', 'Heavenly Bells', 'Sky Bells', 'Silver Bells', 'Marine Bells', 'Jingle Bells', 'Blue Troll', and 'White Troll'.

■ **HOW TO GROW** Sow seeds indoors six to eight weeks before frost danger has passed. Do not cover seeds as they need light during the 14- to 21-day germination period. Transplant plants into the garden two weeks before danger of frost has passed. Plant browallia 6–10in (15–25cm) apart in part shade in a rich, moist, cool, well-drained soil.

CALENDULA OFFICINALIS

POT MARIGOLD, ENGLISH MARIGOLD

THE CRISP FLOWERS of pot marigold are single or double, daisylike or dahlialike, 3–4in (8–10cm) across, and bloom on fuzzy, 8–36in (20–90cm) stems. Calendula's bright blooms of orange, yellow, or apricot are striking in pots or mass plantings, and its petals can be used in teas and as a colorful garnish on food. Tall varieties are 'Kablouna' and 'Pacific Beauty'; dwarf varieties are 'Bon Bon', 'Mandarin', and 'Fiesta Gitana' ('Gypsy Festival') (FS).

■ **HOW TO GROW** Sow seeds outdoors four weeks before the last spring frost, or start seeds indoors four to six weeks earlier. Set plants into the garden two weeks before the last frost. Germination takes 10 to 14 days. Space plants 12–15in (30–38cm) apart.

Calendula grows best when the temperature is below 80°F (26.5°C). It prefers full sun but will grow in light shade as well; soil should be rich and moist. Cut off flowers as they fade in order to prolong blooming. Calendula is susceptible to mildew and aphids; see Insects and Diseases, earlier.

Calendula officinalis

CALLISTEPHUS CHINENSIS

CHINA ASTER

CHINA ASTER HAS single or double blooms of blue, white, lavender, purple, yellow, pink, or red, long cutting stems, and basal foliage. There are several different flower types, including pompon, chrysanthemum, peony, cactus, and plumed forms. Plants grow 6–36in (15–90cm) tall and start blooming in midsummer. Use plants in cuttings gardens, beds, and borders. Tall varieties include 'Perfection', 'Pompon Splendid', and 'Super Princess Symphonie'; medium-sized varieties are 'Crego', 'Early Charm', 'Early Ostrich Plume', 'Fluffy Ruffles', 'Powderpuff' ('Bouquet'), and 'Rainbow'. Dwarf varieties are 'Color Carpet', 'Dwarf Queen', 'Milady', and 'Pinnochio' (FS).

■ **HOW TO GROW** Seeds can either be started outdoors after all danger of frost has passed or started indoors six to eight weeks earlier. Germination takes 10 to 14 days. Space plants, depending on their size, 6–15in (15–38cm) apart in full sun and fertile, rich, moist, well-drained sandy soil. Once aster flowers have been cut or have faded, the plant will not bloom again. Therefore, it is essential to start new plants every two weeks if you want a continuous supply of cut flowers. Planting of early blooming types with others will also give a longer flowering season. Mulch to keep the roots cool and moist. Plants are prone to virus diseases, so select disease-resistant varieties, do not plant China asters near marigolds, and do not plant them in the same spot two years in a row. Also see Diseases, earlier.

Callistephus chinensis 'GEM MIXED'

Capsicum annuum 'HOLIDAY CHEER'

CAPSICUM ANNUUM

ORNAMENTAL PEPPER

ONE OF THE MOST ATTRACTIVE annuals for the garden is really a hot pepper! Tiny white, starry flowers are followed by small fruits that are round, tapered or cone shaped and go through varying shades of white, cream, chartreuse, purple, red, or orange as they mature. The cheery and colorful peppers sit on top of bright green leaves on 4–12in (10–30cm) plants. Ornamental peppers are good in beds, borders, and containers, and are edible as well, either fresh or dried. Varieties include 'Fireworks', 'Holiday Cheer', 'Holiday Flame', 'Holiday Time', 'Masquerade', and 'Red Missile'.

■ **HOW TO GROW** Start seeds indoors six to eight weeks before the last spring frost. Don't cover the seeds which need light during the 21- to 25-day germination period. Plant in full sun or very light shade, 6–9in (15–23cm) apart. Ornamental peppers like a long, hot, humid summer to grow and fruit to their best, and are very heat and drought resistant. Soil should be rich, moist, and well drained. Ornamental peppers are a favorite plant for the winter holiday season as well. To grow them for that time of year, start plants in midspring, allow pots of them to summer outdoors, and bring them inside in fall.

CATHARANTHUS ROSEUS

MADAGASCAR PERIWINKLE, VINCA

P ERIWINKLE HAS LEATHERY, green leaves and waxy, five-petalled flowers of white, pink, or rose on 3–10in (7.5–25cm) spreading or upright plants. Use it in planters, in beds and borders, or as a ground cover, especially where adverse growing conditions exist, as it tolerates heat, drought, and air pollution. Ground-hugging varieties are 'Magic Carpet' and 'Polka Dot'; 'Little Blanche', 'Little Bright Eye', 'Little Delicata', 'Little Pinkie', 'Little Rosie', and 'Little Linda' are upright varieties.

■ **GROWING CONDITIONS** Start seeds indoors 12 weeks before the last frost and cover the seeds which need darkness for the 15- to 20-day germination. Plant periwinkle in full sun or part shade in any well-drained garden soil. Spreading varieties are planted 24in (60cm) apart; upright varieties 6in (15cm) apart.

Catharanthus roseus 'GRAPE COOLER'

CELOSIA CRISTATA

CELOSIA, COCKSCOMB

CELOSIA IS A BIZARRE ANNUAL, both in flower color and shape. This bright and unusual plant actually comes in two different forms. One, the plumed type, has long, feathery flower stalks. The other, the crested or cockscomb type, has round flower heads that are ridged and resemble the comb of a rooster or a brain. All celosia cover a rainbow of colors so bright that they need to be used with care in the garden. Red, rose, pink, yellow, cream, apricot, orange, gold, or salmon shades are available.

Celosia are available in dwarf varieties 6in (15cm) high for borders and edgings, and tall varieties 30in (75cm) high that are perfect for the back of the border or cut flowers. Plumed varieties are 'Apricot Brandy' (AAS), 'Castle Pink' (AAS), 'Century Mixed' (AAS, RHS), 'Dwarf Fairy Fountains' (RHS), 'New Look' (AAS), 'Forest Fire', and 'Geisha'. The best crested celosia is 'Jewel Box' (RHS).

■ **HOW TO GROW** Seeds may be sown outdoors after all danger of frost has passed, but for best results, start seeds indoors four weeks earlier. Germination takes 10 to 15 days. If plants are set into the garden too early, they will flower prematurely, set seed, and be ruined. Plant celosia in full sun, 6–18in (15–45cm) apart, in rich, well-drained soil. Celosia is very tolerant of heat and drought.

Celosia cristata 'JEWEL BOX YELLOW'

Centaurea Cyanus

CENTAUREA CYANUS

CORNFLOWER, BACHELOR'S BUTTON

CORNFLOWER'S BLOOMS ARE DOUBLE, frilly, ruffled, or tufted. They are primarily blue but may be pink, rose, lavender, or white, and bloom on top of wiry stems and long, thin foliage. Taller varieties are good for the back of the border; shorter types are perfect as edgings. They are also long-lasting cut flowers and excellent candidates for drying. Cornflower or bachelor's button grows up to 12–36in (30–90cm) tall. 'Blue Boy' is a tall variety; 'Polka Dot', a medium-sized variety; and 'Jubilee Gem', a short variety.

■ **HOW TO GROW** Seeds or plants may be set into the garden in midspring as soon as the soil can be worked. For earlier bloom, start seeds indoors four weeks before moving plants outdoors.

Germination takes 7 to 14 days, and seeds must be completely covered as they need darkness to germinate. Where winters are mild, seeds can be sown in fall for early spring bloom. Cornflowers are not long-blooming plants, so seeds should be sown successively every two weeks through spring and summer for a continuous supply of garden and indoor color.

Set plants 6–24in (15–60cm) apart in full sun and light, rich, dry soil for preference, although they will tolerate poor soil. Keep blooms cut to prolong blooming time as long as possible. Cornflowers have a tendency to be affected by rust; see Diseases, earlier.

Cleome Hasslerana 'WHITE QUEEN'

CLEOME HASSLERANA

SPIDER FLOWER

NAMED FOR THE SHAPE OF ITS PETALS, spider flower has 6–7in (15–18cm) flowers with long stamens and strongly fragrant florets of white, rose, pink, or lavender. Compound leaves have five to seven leaflets and two spines at the base of each leaf. Conspicuous seed pods are long and slim. At the back of the border or in a large bed, the waving 3–6ft (1–2m) stems of spider flower are most attractive. 'Colour Fountain' and 'Queen' mixture are the best-known spider flowers.

■ **HOW TO GROW** Sow seeds outdoors after all danger of frost has passed, or start seeds indoors four to six weeks earlier. Germination takes 10 to 14 days. Plant spider flower 2–3ft (0.6–1m) apart in average to infertile soil, in a warm spot that receives full sun. It will withstand high heat, and is very drought resistant.

COLEUS X HYBRIDUS

COLEUS

COLEUS HAS FOLIAGE WITH splashy combinations of green, red, chartreuse, white, gold, bronze, scarlet, ivory, orange, salmon, rose, copper, yellow, apricot, pink, and purple. The leaves are edged, blotched, or patterned in contrasting colors, and the edges may be lacy, smooth, fringed, wavy, or toothed. Coleus may bloom in late summer, with spikes of tiny blue or lavender flowers, but plants are grown for the foliage. Use coleus in beds, borders, or containers. Plants vary in height from 6–36in (15–90cm). Popular varieties include the 'Carefree', 'Dragon', 'Fiji', 'Poncho', 'Rainbow', 'Saber', and 'Wizard' series, and 'Festive Dance'.

■ **HOW TO GROW** Start seeds indoors six to eight weeks before the last spring frost. Do not cover them as they need light to germinate, which will take 10 to 15 days. Coleus can also be propagated by rooting stem cuttings. Coleus prefers part to heavy shade and should be spaced 10–12in (25–30cm) apart. Soil should be rich and moist. Flowers may be left on the plants as they form, although removing them will extend the period of bright foliage color. Coleus is susceptible to aphids and mealybugs; see Insects, earlier.

Coleus x hybridus 'ROSE WIZARD'

Coreopsis tinctoria GRANDIFLORA

COREOPSIS TINCTORIA

CALLIOPSIS

CALLIOPSIS HAS DAISYLIKE, 1¼in (3cm) flowers that can be bright red, yellow, pink, or purple, some solid colored, some banded. Slender and wiry stems are 8–36in (20–90cm) tall. Good varieties to look for are 'Early Sunrise' (AAS, FS) and 'Sunray' (FS).

■ **HOW TO GROW** Seeds can be sown outdoors in midspring, but earlier flowering will result by starting seeds indoors six to eight weeks before outdoor plant-ing. Seeds germinate in 5 to 10 days and need light to germinate. Transplant carefully as calliopsis resents having its roots disturbed; space plants 8–12in (20–30cm) apart. Caliopsis likes full sun and light, dry, infertile, sandy soil with excellent drainage. Keep flowers clipped as they fade to keep plants neat and producing more flowers.

COSMOS

COSMOS FILLS THE GARDEN with clusters of bushy plants with slender stems, and single or double daisylike flowers that have wide and serrated petals. There are two cosmos species. *C. bipinnatus* is known as the Sensation type and is 3–4ft (1–1.3m) tall with lacy foliage. Flowers are 3–6in (7.5–15cm) across and lavender, pink, or white. 'Sensation Mixed' and 'Day-dream' are good varieties. *C. sulphureus* is called the Klondyke type. Its foliage is denser and broader, plants are generally shorter, and flowers are yellow, red, gold, or orange. Good varieties include 'Bright Lights', 'Diablo', 'Sunny Red' (AAS, FS), 'Sunny Gold', 'Sunny Orange', and 'Sunny Yellow'. Taller types are excellent for the back of the border or grown as cut flowers; shorter varieties find a place in mid-border or mass plantings.

■ **HOW TO GROW** Seeds may be sown outdoors after all danger of frost has passed, or started indoors five to seven weeks before the last frost. Germination takes 5 to 10 days. Plant cosmos 9–24in (23–60cm) apart, depending on their ultimate size, in full sun and in a warm spot. Soil should be dry and infertile. To keep plants neat, cut off faded flowers. Tall types may need staking.

Cosmos bipinnatus 'SENSATION'

Dahlia 'TED'S CHOICE'

DAHLIA

Dahlias bloom in all colors except blue, in single daisylike, double daisylike, informal, quill, anemone, cactus, peony, ball, or pompon forms. They are available in varieties from 1–3ft (0.3–1m) tall which include 'Cactus Flowered', 'Dahl Face', 'Figaro', 'Red,-skin' (AAS, ABT, FS), 'Rigoletto', 'Showpiece', 'Sunny Red', and 'Sunny Yellow' (FS). Dahlias provide season-long color in beds, borders, and containers, and make excellent cut flowers as well.

■ **HOW TO GROW** Dahlias are grown from either seeds or tubers. Most of those grown from seed have unpredictable colors, although flower form and plant size can be known in advance. Tubers provide the same plant in the same color, year after year. Whether dahlias are started from seeds or tubers, new tubers form during the growing season that can be dug after the first fall frost, stored indoors over the winter, and replanted the following spring.

To grow dahlias from seeds, start them indoors four to six weeks before the last frost. Germination takes 5 to 10 days. Space plants 8–24in (20–60cm) apart, in light, rich, moist, fertile soil with excellent drainage. Dahlias prefer full sun but will grow and bloom well in light shade.

Tall varieties may need to be staked, and all types will benefit from having their faded flowers removed to encourage neatness and further bloom. If very large blooms are desired, side buds can be removed. Since they are prone to a variety of insects and fungal diseases, regular spraying with a fungicide and general insecticide is advised.

To store tubers over the winter, wait until the frost has blackened the tops. Dig the dahlias and store them in a cool, dry place away from light. Check them from time to time to make sure they are not drying out. If they start to grow, they are receiving too much light and/or heat.

58

DIANTHUS

PINKS, CARNATION, SWEET WILLIAM

THE DIANTHUS GENUS is a large one, with members known as pinks, Sweet William and carnation. Flowers are red, white, pink, rose, or lilac and most have petals with lacy edgings that look as if they were cut with pinking shears. All have a delicious fragrance, reminiscent of cloves or other spices. Plant them where their aroma can be enjoyed, in rock gardens, rock walls, beds, or borders, or grow for cut flowers.

D. *barbatus*, Sweet William, grows 12in (30cm) high and has blooms that appear in dense, round clusters. D. *chinensis*, China pink, grows 6–18in (15–45cm) tall, with single- or double-frilled, flat-topped flowers. Foliage is grasslike and gray-green. Popular varieties include 'China Doll', 'Fire Carpet' (RHS), 'Magic Charms' (AAS), 'Princess', 'Snowfire' (AAS), 'Telstar' (FS), 'Telstar Picotee' (AAS), and 'Telstar Crimson' (FS). D. *caryophyllus*, carnation, is 8–24in (20–60cm) tall and has double-frilled flowers. Try 'Scarlet Luminette' (AAS), 'Crimson Knight' (FS), or other members of the 'Knight' series (RHS).

■ **HOW TO GROW** Dianthus seeds should be started indoors six to eight weeks before the last frost; germination takes 5 to 10 days. Space plants 6–12in (15–30cm) apart in full sun and light, rich, alkaline, well-drained soil. Cut back plants after they bloom to encourage further flowering. Dianthus prefer cool to moderate climate and high humidity. Some dianthus, particularly the newer hybrids, may be perennial in areas where winters do not go below 0°F (−18°C.)

Dianthus barbatus

Dianthus caryophyllus WITH MUMS

Dianthus chinensis 'TELSTAR PICOTEE' (AAS)

GAILLARDIA PULCHELLA

GAILLARDIA, BLANKET FLOWER

FLOWERS OF GAILLARDIA are double, ball shaped, 2½in (6cm) across, and in a brilliant color range of red, bronze, butterscotch, and maroon, with fringed petals tipped in yellow. Neat plants grow 10–24in (25–60cm) tall. Plant them in beds or borders, or grow for cut flowers.

■ **HOW TO GROW** Seeds may be sown outdoors after all danger of frost has passed or started indoors four to six weeks earlier. Germination takes 15 to 20 days. Plant them a distance apart equal to their ultimate height. Soil should be light, sandy, infertile, and well drained. Gaillardia prefers full sun and is heat and drought tolerant. Remove flowers as they fade. In humid, cool areas, watch for signs of fungus disease; see Diseases, earlier.

Gaillardia pulchella

Gazania rigens 'MARGUERITE'

GAZANIA RIGENS

GAZANIA, TREASURE FLOWER

GAZANIA FLOWERS ARE single and daisylike, in tones of yellow, gold, orange, cream, pink, or red. Some are striped, some have yellow centers, and some have dark centers. Stems 8–10in (20–25cm) tall rise above basal leaves that are dark green on top and felty white or silver on the undersides. Gazania can be used in the garden as edgings, bedding plants, ground covers, or in containers. The flowers close up at night or on cloudy days. Varieties include 'Chansonette', 'Daybreak', 'Mini Star Tangerine' (AAS, FS), 'Mini Star Yellow' (FS), and 'Sundance'.

■ **HOW TO GROW** Start seeds indoors four to six weeks before the last spring frost or sow seeds outdoors after frost danger has passed. Seeds must be covered as they need darkness to germinate, which takes 8 to 14 days. Plant gazania 8–10in (20–25cm) apart in full sun and light, sandy soil. Gazania is heat and drought tolerant. To keep plants tidy and productive, cut blooms as they fade. Gazania can be dug out of the garden in late summer, potted up and brought indoors for several more months of color.

Gerbera Jamesonii 'HAPPIPOT'

GERBERA JAMESONII

GERBERA, TRANSVAAL DAISY, BARBERTON DAISY

DAISYLIKE GERBERA FLOWERS bloom singly on leaf-less stems, and are up to 5in (12.5cm) across in shades of orange, red, pink, white, yellow, salmon, or lavender. Popular varieties are compact and grow up to 12in (30cm) tall. Foliage hugs the ground and is dark green, textured, and with white woolly undersides. Gerbera is a perennial in frost-free areas. Plant it in beds, borders, containers, grow it for cut flowers, or keep indoors as a flowering houseplant. Varieties include 'Double Parade Mix', 'Happipot', and 'Mardi Gras Mixed'.

■ **HOW TO GROW** Start fresh seeds indoors 20 weeks before the last spring frost. When sowing, place the sharp end of the seed down, but do not cover it completely as it needs light to germinate, which takes 15 to 25 days. Space gerbera 12–15in (30–38cm) apart in full sun and moist, very rich, fertile, slightly acid soil. Make sure the crown is not planted below soil level. Keep faded flowers removed to keep plants in good condition and blooming heavily. Be on the watch for signs of slugs and snails; see Insects, earlier.

Gerbera Jamesonii

Gomphrena globosa

GOMPHRENA

Globe Amaranth

GLOBE AMARANTH HAS round, mounded, papery, cloverlike flowers. Plants grow 30in (75cm) tall and have long cutting stems. Globe amaranth is at home in massed plantings and borders, and as a cut or dried flower. *G. globosa* has blooms that come in a range of colors from purple through lavender, rose, pink, orange, yellow, and white. *G. Haageana* has red bracts and yellow flowers.

■ **HOW TO GROW** Start seeds indoors six to eight weeks before the last frost. Germination takes 15 to 20 days. Cover seeds well as they need darkness to germinate. Speedier germination can be achieved by soaking the seeds in water before sowing. Seeds can be sown outside after all danger of frost has passed, but the plants will bloom later in the summer. Set plants 10–15in (25–38cm) apart in full sun. Globe amaranth tolerates drought and heat. Soil should be sandy, light, fertile, and well drained. To dry flowers, cut blooms before they are fully open and hang them upside down in an airy, cool, dry spot.

Sunflower

PLANTS WITH LARGE, coarse, hairy, somewhat sticky leaves are topped with large, single, daisylike yellow flowers with centers of dark red, purple, or brown, or double flowers of gold. There are dwarf forms of sunflower that grow to only 15in (38cm), but the traditional, well-known plant reaches 4–6ft (1.3–2m) or more. Dwarf sunflower is grown as a bedding plant, tall sunflower as a novelty. Both attract birds and are good plants for children's gardens. Select from 'Autumn Beauty', 'Color Fashion', 'Italian White', 'Sunbright', 'Sunburst Mixed', 'Sunspot', or 'Teddy Bear'.

■ **HOW TO GROW** Sow seeds outdoors after all danger of spring frost has passed. Seeds can be started indoors and will germinate in 10 to 14 days, but sunflower grows so fast that this is not necessary. Plant 2–4ft (0.6–1.3m) apart in full sun and a light, dry, infertile, well-drained soil. Stake to support tall plants. Sunflowers grow best where summers are hot.

Helianthus annuus 'PYGMY DWARF'

Helichrysum bracteatum 'GOLD BIKINI'

HELICHRYSUM BRACTEATUM

STRAWFLOWER

Branched plants grow 12–30in (30–75cm) tall and have narrow leaves and wiry stems. Flowers, which are made up of bracts rather than petals, are stiff, brightly colored and papery, in shades of red, salmon, purple, yellow, pink, or white. Although it can be used as a garden plant or cut flower, strawflower is usually grown for drying. 'Hot Bikini' (FS) and other members of the 'Bikini' series are good varieties to plant, as is 'Frosted Sulphur/Silvery Rose'.

■ **HOW TO GROW** Seeds can be sown outdoors after all danger of frost has passed, but better results will be achieved by starting seeds indoors four to six weeks earlier. Do not cover the seeds which need light during the 7 to 10-day germination. Plant in full sun, 9–15in (23–38cm) apart, in porous, fertile, well-drained soil. Strawflower thrives where summers are hot and dry.

To dry flowers, cut them just before the center petals open, strip off the foliage and hang the flowers upside down in a shaded area.

HIBISCUS MOSCHEUTOS

HIBISCUS, ROSE MALLOW

SHRUBBY PLANTS OF varying heights from 18in–6ft (45cm–2m) are filled during summer with large, usually single, five-petalled, pink, white, or red flowers with a prominent tubular structure protruding from the center of the flower. The stems are downy and the leaves are hairy. 'Dixie Belle' and 'Disco Belle' are short varieties while 'Southern Belle' is tall. All are useful as hedges or accents, especially where an exotic or tropical look is desired.

■ **HOW TO GROW** Seeds may be sown outdoors after all danger of frost has passed, or sown indoors six to eight weeks earlier. Seeds have a hard coating. Either clip the seeds with a knife or scissors, or soak them in water until they sink, when they are ready to be planted. Germination takes 15 to 30 days. Plant dwarf hibiscus a distance apart equal to its ultimate height. Tall hibiscus should be planted a distance apart equal to about two-thirds of its ultimate height. Hibiscus like full sun or light shade and rich, well-drained, moist soil. It tolerates high temperatures in summer as long as it is kept well watered.

Hibiscus Moscheutos 'DISCO BELLE WHITE'

Hunnemannia fumariifolia

HUNNEMANNIA FUMARIIFOLIA

MEXICAN TULIP POPPY

THIS ANNUAL LOOKS LIKE a cross between a tulip and a poppy. Flowers are yellow, 3in (7.5cm) across, and ruffle-edged. Downy, smooth, finely divided, fernlike, blue-green leaves cover the 2ft (0.6m) plant. Use it as a cut flower as well as in the flower border. 'Sunlight' is the most popular variety.

■ **HOW TO GROW** Sow seeds outdoors after all danger of frost has passed, or start seeds indoors four to six weeks earlier. Germination takes 15 to 20 days. Mexican tulip poppy dislikes transplanting, so grow it in individual peat pots to lessen transplanting shock. Plants should be set 9–12in (23–30cm) apart in a warm location and full sun. Soil should be light, dry, infertile, well drained, and slightly alkaline.

IBERIS

CANDYTUFT

ANNUAL CANDYTUFT, like its perennial cousin, is excellent for borders, edgings, and rock gardens. *I. amara*, rocket candytuft, grows 18–20in (45–50cm) tall and is covered with large, upright, cone-shaped spikes of fragrant, glistening white flowers resembling loose hyacinths. Leaves are coarsely toothed. This species is excellent as a cut flower. 'Hyacinth Flowered' is the popular variety. *I. umbellata*, globe candytuft, is 8–10in (20–25cm) high and dome shaped, and has narrow leaves. Round clusters of flowers are pink, crimson, rose, carmine, lavender, or white, with no fragrance. 'Fairy Mixed' and 'Red Flash' (ABT) are well-known varieties.

■ **HOW TO GROW** Sow seeds outdoors after all danger of frost has passed, or, for earlier bloom, start seeds indoors six to eight weeks earlier. Germination takes 10 to 15 days. Plant candytuft 6–10in (15–25cm) apart in full sun and average, well-drained garden soil. Candytuft does best in cool climates. After blooms fade, shearing the plants will encourage further flowering.

Iberis umbellata

Impatiens Balsamina

IMPATIENS BALSAMINA

BALSAM

BALSAM BLOOMS ARE WAXY, borne close to the stem, and can be single but are usually double. They look like roses or camellias in shades of white, pink, red, purple, lavender, salmon, or yellow, and are sometimes solid colored, sometimes spotted. Plants grow 10–36in (25–90cm) tall and are clothed with pointed, toothed leaves. A favorite in Victorian gardens, balsam is still used in beds, borders, and planters.

■ **HOW TO GROW** Seeds may be sown outdoors after all danger of frost has passed or, for earlier bloom, start seeds indoors six to eight weeks earlier. Germination takes 8 to 14 days. Plant balsam 6–15in (15–38cm) apart in full sun or part shade in a rich, fertile, moist, well-drained soil. Balsam is heat tolerant.

IMPATIENS 'NEW GUINEA'

NEW GUINEA IMPATIENS

DISCOVERED IN THE 1970s by a plant expedition to New Guinea and brought back to the western world, New Guinea impatiens have become extremely popular. It is not so much their flowers, which bloom in shades of lavender, orange, pink, red, salmon, and purple, but rather their showy leaves that are variegated in green, yellow, and cream that make them a welcomed addition to the garden. Plants grow 12–24in (30–60cm) high. New Guinea impatiens are perfect for beds, borders, hanging baskets, and planters, and can be grown indoors. Look for the 'Sunshine' series, 'Sweet Sue', and 'Tango' (AAS).

■ **HOW TO GROW** New Guinea impatiens can be propagated by rooting tip cuttings; 'Sweet Sue' and 'Tango' can be grown from seeds. Start seeds indoors 12 to 16 weeks before the last frost. Temperatures must be very warm during the 14- to 28-day germination period. Only about 50 per cent of the seeds will normally germinate, so sow more heavily than usual. Set plants outdoors, 12in (30cm) apart, in part to full sun and very rich, moist, well-drained soil. Mulch plants right after they are set into the ground as cool soil is needed for best growth.

Impatiens 'New Guinea'

Impatients Wallerana 'SUPER ELFIN ROSE'

IMPATIENS WALLERANA

IMPATIENS

IMPATIENS ARE LOVED for their rainbow of flower colors, variety of sizes, nonstop bloom from spring to fall frost, easy care, shade tolerance, uniform habit and dependability. Impatiens grow from the shortest of ground covers to tall, mounded plants reaching 18in (45cm). Most flowers are flat, 1–2in (2.5–5cm) across, and single with five petals, although there are double varieties. Flower colors include white, pink, salmon, orange, scarlet, red, and violet, plus there are bicolors that have white, starlike centers. Impatiens are used under trees, in shady beds and borders, and in container plantings.

There are many varieties of impatiens, including the 'Accent', 'Dazzler', 'Duet' (RHS), 'Futura', 'Mini', 'Novette', 'Princess', 'Rosette' and 'Super Elfin' series, all of which are available in a wide choice of colors. Other good varieties are 'Orange Blitz' (AAS) and 'Starbright' (FS).

■ **HOW TO GROW** Start seeds indoors 10 to 14 weeks before the last spring frost. Germination takes 14 days. Impatiens can also be propagated by rooting stem cuttings. Space plants 10–12in (25–30cm) apart for the dwarf types and 18in (45cm) apart for tall varieties. Soil should be rich, slightly moist, and well drained. Impatiens will perform well in a wide range of temperatures, including high heat, especially when the humidity is high. Do not overfeed impatiens as this will cause them to stop blooming. Flowers fall cleanly as they fade, reducing maintenance.

IPOMOEA

Morning Glory

THE MORNING GLORY and its many relatives are a large group of annual vines which quickly grow to 10–30ft (3–9m) per year to cover and screen fences, trellises or other areas where privacy is needed. Showy flowers are funnel shaped. Morning glories can also be used in hanging baskets. *I. alba*, moon vine, has white, fragrant flowers that open in the evening. *I. X multifida*, cardinal climber, has red flowers. *I. Quamoclit*, cypress vine, has flowers of red, pink, or white. The well-known vining morning glories belong to one of three genera: *I.Nil, purpurea*, and *tricolor*. Flowers are blue, purple, pink, red, or white, opening in the morning and fading by afternoon.

■ **HOW TO GROW** Seeds can be started indoors in individual pots four to six weeks before the last frost, or outdoors after frost danger has passed. Germination takes five to seven days. Seeds have a hard coat; either nick them with a file or tiny scissors or soak them for 24 hours in warm water.

Set plants 12–18in (30–45cm) apart in full sun and in light, infertile, dry, well-drained soil. A trellis or other support will be needed.

Ipomoea tricolor 'HEAVENLY BLUE'

Kochia scoparia forma *trichophylla*

KOCHIA SCOPARIA FORMA *TRICHOPHYLLA*

SUMMER CYPRESS, BURNING BUSH

FOR MOST OF THE SUMMER, kochia adds little to the garden, but in early autumn, it starts to turn bright cherry red and becomes a real attraction. Looking like a conifer, the plant is dense, globe shaped, 3ft (1m) tall, and has narrow, feathery foliage. The greenish flowers are insignificant and all but invisible. Try summer cypress as a hedge or garden novelty.

■ **HOW TO GROW** Seeds can either be sown outdoors after all danger of frost has passed, or started inside four to six weeks earlier. Do not cover seeds which need light during the 10- to 15-day germination period. Space plants 18–24in (45–60cm) apart in full sun and dry soil with excellent drainage. Plants grow best in hot weather. To keep them in symmetrical shape, they can easily be sheared. Seeds drop easily and quickly sprout, which can be somewhat of a nuisance.

LATHYRUS ODORATUS

SWEET PEA

SWEET PEAS COME in two types; annual vines that climb to 6ft (2m), and bushy plants that reach 2½ft (0.75m) tall. The flowers are deliciously fragrant, in purple, rose, red, white, pink, and blue, some solid colored, some bicolored. Varieties include 'Bijou', 'Lady Fairbairn' (RHS), 'Maggie May', 'North Shore' (RHS), 'Pagentry' (RHS), 'Penine Floss' (RHS), 'Red Ensign' (RHS), 'Royal Family', 'Royal Flush' (RHS), 'Snoopea' (RHS), 'Supersnoop', 'Superstar' (RHS), and 'Wiltshire Ripple' (RHS).

■ **HOW TO GROW** Sow seeds outdoors in early spring as soon as the soil can be worked; in mild areas, seeds can be sown in fall for early bloom the following spring. Seeds can also be started indoors four to six weeks before outdoor planting, but sowing in individual pots is recommended as sweet pea doesn't like to be transplanted. Soak the seeds in water for 24 hours before planting, or file the hard seed coat to hasten germination, which takes 10 to 14 days. Cover seeds as they need darkness to germinate. Plant bushy types 15in (38cm) apart; vining types should be planted 6–8in (15–20cm) apart. Provide a trellis or other support for the climbers, and give both types full sun. Soil should be deeply prepared, rich, moist, and slightly alkaline. Mulch the soil to keep it cool and damp. Sweet pea does best where it's cool and away from drying winds. Keep faded flowers picked to prolong flowering.

Lathyrus odoratus

Lavatera trimestris 'MONT BLANC' (FS)

LAVATERA TRIMESTRIS

MALLOW

PINK, RED OR WHITE 4in (10cm) blooms are cuplike, resembling hollyhocks, and form in the upper leaf axils. Leaves are dark green and maplelike, and often turn bronze in cool weather. Plants have hairy stems and grow 2–3ft (0.6–1m) tall. For borders, hedges, backgrounds, or screens, lavatera is a good choice. The varieties 'Mont Blanc' (FS), 'Mont Rose', 'Silver Cup' (FS), and 'Splendens' are best known.

■ **HOW TO GROW** Lavatera seeds can be started indoors in early spring, but they are hard to transplant. Therefore, it is better to sow seeds in place outdoors in midspring. In mild areas, seeds can be planted outdoors in fall to germinate and grow the following spring. Germination takes 15 to 20 days. Plant lavatera in full sun, 15–24in (38–60cm) apart, in dry, well-drained soil. Keep faded flowers picked to prolong blooming. Lavatera performs best where nights are cool.

LOBELIA ERINUS

LOBELIA

GROWN PRIMARILY FOR its outstanding multitude of small blue to purple flowers, lobelia also has varieties with white or pink blooms. Plants grow 4in (10cm) tall and spread to cover an area 10in (25cm) across. Use for edgings, borders, ground covers, rock gardens, and containers. 'Blue Moon', 'Cascade', 'Crystal Palace', 'Rosamund', and 'White Lady' are popular varieties.

■ **HOW TO GROW** Start seeds indoors 10 to 12 weeks before the last frost. Do not cover the seeds and provide them with a warm (75°F, 24°C) environment during germination, which takes 15 to 20 days. Plant lobelia 8–10in (20–25cm) apart in full sun or part shade in rich, moist, well-drained soil. Lobelia does best where summers are cool. Flowers fall cleanly as they fade. Leggy plants can be cut back to encourage compactness and heavier bloom.

Lobelia Erinus 'BRIGHT EYES'

Lobularia maritima

LOBULARIA MARITIMA
SWEET ALYSSUM

DOMED CLUSTERS OF TINY, sweetly scented flowers of white, rose, lavender, or purple cover plants that grow 3–4in (7.5–10cm) tall and 12in (30cm) across. Foliage is linear and needlelike. Choose sweet alyssum for borders, edgings, or containers, especially where its fragrance will be appreciated. Good varieties include 'Carpet of Snow', 'Rosie O'Day' (AAS), 'Royal Carpet', 'Snow Cloth', 'Snow Crystals' (FS), and 'Wonderland' (FS).

■ **HOW TO GROW** Seeds may be sown outdoors several weeks' before the last expected frost, or started indoors four to six weeks earlier. Do not cover seeds as light is necessary for germination, which takes 8 to 15 days. Seeds are very prone to damping off; see Diseases, earlier. Set plants 10–12in (25–30cm) apart, in full sun or partial shade and average, well-drained soil. Sweet alyssum prefers to be kept moist but will tolerate drought. Although it prefers cool nights, it will grow successfully, if not as floriferously, in hot areas. Flowers fall cleanly as they fade, and plants can be cut back if they become leggy to encourage compactness and further bloom.

MATTHIOLA INCANA
STOCK

STOCK GROWS 12–18in (30–45cm) tall and produces stiff spikes of cross-shaped single or double flowers. Blooms are red, white, cream, pink, rose, blue, or purple over narrow blue-gray leaves. Some stocks produce only one bloom spike and are known as columnar types; others are multibranching and more compact. All are biennials grown as annuals. Stock is a pretty plant for a formal garden and a marvelous cut flower, but one of its best assets is its fragrance, especially in the evening. Stock is often classified as seven-week or ten-week, which is the amount of time after germination that it takes for plants to bloom. Good varieties include 'Trysomic 7-Week', 'Giant Imperial', 'Midget', 'Dwarf 10-Week', 'Stockpot', and 'Beauty of Nice', which are branching types, and 'Giant Excelsior', which is a columnar type.

■ **HOW TO GROW** Plants can be set into the garden in midspring about four weeks before the last expected frost. Start seeds indoors six to eight weeks earlier. Do not cover the seeds as light is needed for germination, which takes 7 to 10 days. Space stock 12–15in (30–38cm) apart in full sun and light, sandy, rich, fertile, moist soil. Stock does best in cool climates. Keep flowers picked to prolong blooming. For all double flowers, select the seedlings with the palest green leaves.

Matthiola incana 'WHITE CHRISTMAS'

Mimulus x hybridus

MIMULUS X HYBRIDUS

MONKEY FLOWER

THE MONKEY FLOWER'S BLOOMS are tubular and two lipped, and look like a cross between a petunia and a snapdragon. Blooms are yellow, gold, or red, often flecked with a contrasting color, and reminiscent of a monkey's face. Plants grow 6–10in (15–25cm) high, and are best in beds, borders, or containers. Varieties include 'Calypso' (RHS), 'Malibu', and 'Velvet.

■ **HOW TO GROW** Seeds should be started indoors six to eight weeks before the outdoor planting date. Do not cover seeds which need 13 hours of light per day to germinate, which takes 7 to 14 days. Plant out-doors in early to midspring as soon as the soil can be worked, 6in (15cm) apart in rich, moist, well-drained soil. Mimulus does best in part shade or shade, although it will grow in full sun if temperatures are cool and humidity is high.

MIRABILIS JALAPA

FOUR O'CLOCK

HEAVILY BRANCHED, 18–36in (45–90cm) plants have trumpet- or funnel-shaped fragrant flowers of white, red, yellow, pink, or violet. Blooms are solid, mottled, striped, veined, or splashed with contrasting colors. Flowers open in the afternoon and stay open until the following morning. When skies are cloudy, the flowers remain open all day. For the back of the border or as a hedge, the four o'clock's lovely flowers are an asset even though the plant itself is not very attractive.

■ **HOW TO GROW** Sow seeds outdoors after all danger of frost has passed, or, for better results, start seeds indoors four to six weeks earlier. Germination takes 7 to 10 days. Space plants 12–18in (30–45cm) apart in full sun and light, fertile, well-drained soil. Four o'clock tolerates poor soil and summer heat, although it will do well where temperatures are cool. Although roots may be dug and stored over the winter in the same manner as dahlias, four o'clock is so easy to grow and reseeds so readily that this is not necessary.

Mirabilis Jalapa

Nemesia strumosa

NEMESIA STRUMOSA

POUCH NEMESIA

RACEMES OF TUBULAR, cuplike flowers that have pouches at their bases bloom in white, yellow, bronze, blue, scarlet, orange, gold, pink, cream, and lavender, in solids and bicolors. The leaves are attractive and finely toothed. The 8–18in (20–45cm) plants are useful in rock gardens, edgings, borders, and containers. Varieties include 'Carnival Mixed', 'Mello', and 'Tapestry'.

■ **HOW TO GROW** Sow seeds outdoors after all danger of frost has passed, or, for better results, start seeds indoors four to six weeks earlier. Seeds must be completely covered as they need darkness to germinate, which takes 7 to 14 days. Plant 6in (15cm) apart in full sun or light shade and rich, moist, well-drained soil. Pinch back when planting into the garden to induce bushiness. Nemesia grows best where summers are cool and the humidity is low.

NEMOPHILA MENZIESII

BABY BLUE EYES

NEMOPHILA MENZIESII

BABY BLUE EYES

BABY BLUE EYES has decorative, heavily cut leaves and bell-shaped, highly fragrant flowers that are usually blue with white centers. Trailing stems spread to fill a space 12in (30cm) across and 6in (15cm) high. For rock gardens, ground covers, wildflower gardens, or beds, baby blue eyes is a good choice for its glorious flowers.

■ **HOW TO GROW** Sow seeds outdoors in early spring as soon as the soil can be worked. In warm areas, seeds can be sown in fall for color the following spring. Seeds can also be started inside six weeks before the outdoor planting date, provided a 55°F (13°C) temperature can be maintained during germination, which takes 7 to 12 days. Set plants 8–12in (20–30cm) apart in full sun or, preferably, light shade. Soil should be light, sandy, and well drained. Baby blue eyes self-sows readily, so it acts almost as a perennial in cool areas, where it grows best. It also benefits from being sheltered from the wind.

Nemophila Menziesii

Nicotiana alata 'DOMINO'

NICOTIANA ALATA

FLOWERING TOBACCO

FLOWERING TOBACCO IS AN extremely pretty relative of the commercially grown tobacco (*N. Tabacum*). Modern varieties are 10–18in (25–45cm) tall, compact, and have trumpet-shaped flowers of yellow, purple, green, red, pink, or white that grow in loose bunches. Leaves are fuzzy and slightly sticky. Flowering tobacco is effective when mass planted or in a border. Good varieties are the 'Domino' and 'Sensation' series.

■ **HOW TO GROW** Seeds can be sown outdoors after all danger of frost has passed, but for earlier bloom, start seeds indoors six to eight weeks before. Germination takes 10 to 20 days; seeds should not be covered as they need light to germinate. Nicotiana flourishes in full sun or part shade. Space plants 10–12in (25–30cm) apart in rich, well-drained soil. Nicotiana will tolerate heat as long as the humidity is high and the plants are well watered. Keep plants neat by cutting off dead flower stalks. Nicotiana freely reseeds.

NIEREMBERGIA HIPPOMANICA

CUPFLOWER

CUP-SHAPED, BLUE VIOLET blooms cover 6–12in (15–30cm) mounded plants that have hairy, fernlike leaves. Use cupflower in beds, borders, as edgings, or in rock gardens. 'Purple Robe' is the best-known variety.

■ **HOW TO GROW** Start seeds indoors 10 to 12 weeks before the last spring frost. Germination takes 15 to 20 days. Plant 6–9in (15–23cm) apart in full sun to light shade in light, moist, well-drained soil.

Nierembergia hippomanica 'PURPLE ROBE'

Nigella damascena 'MISS JECKYL'

NIGELLA DAMASCENA

LOVE-IN-A-MIST

LOVE-IN-A-MIST HAS flowers of pink, blue, white, and purple which are shaped like cornflowers, with tapered petals and prominent stamens. Blooms sit within collars of fine, threadlike, misty foliage on thin, many-branched, 12–24in (30–60cm) stems. Pungent, round, pine-green seed pods with red markings are used to flavor food and taste somewhat like nutmeg. Love-in-a-mist is sometimes called fennel flower. The cut flowers are used in fresh arrangements; the seed pods in dried arrangements. 'Persian Jewels' and 'Miss Jeckyl' are popular varieties.

■ **HOW TO GROW** Love-in-a-mist has a short blooming period, so seeds must be sown sucessively outdoors from early spring to early summer for continuous bloom. Seeds can be started indoors four to six weeks before planting outdoors, but as love-in-a-mist resents transplanting, sow in individual pots and transplant with care. Germination takes 10 to 15 days. Final spacing should be 8–10in (20–25cm) apart. Plant in full sun and moist garden soil with excellent drainage. Love-in-a-mist prefers cool weather and is tolerant of frost.

PAPAVER

POPPY

POPPIES HAVE SINGLE or double, crêpe-paper-like flowers with large black centers. Stems are branching and wiry over deeply cut leaves. *P. nudicale*, Iceland poppy, has flowers of white, pink, yellow, orange, or red on 1ft (0.3m) stems. *P. Rhoeas*, corn poppy or Shirley poppy, grows to 3ft (1m) and has flowers of red, purple, or white.

■ **HOW TO GROW** Seeds can be sown outdoors in either late fall or early spring. Seeds may also be started indoors, but cool (55°F, 13°C) temperatures are required and the plants are difficult to transplant. Cover seeds completely as they need darkness to germinate, which takes 10 to 15 days. Sow Shirley poppy seeds successively every two weeks during spring and early summer to ensure continual blooming. Set plants 9–12in (23–30cm) apart in full sun and rich, dry soil with excellent drainage.

Papaver Rhoeas

Papaver nudicale

PELARGONIUM

GERANIUM

THE GERANIUM IS one of the most popular garden flowers for beds, borders, and containers. The garden geranium, *P. X hortorum*, has round heads of single or double flowers that can measure up to 5in (12.5cm) across and bloom on top of leafless 8–24in (20–60cm) stems. Flower colors are white, pink, rose, salmon, coral, lavender, or red. These are known as zonal geraniums, and some of the heart-shaped leaves do have brown or black zoning, while others are solid green. Geraniums are available in varieties propagated by either cuttings or seeds. Cutting types do better in containers, and seed types, which are more tolerant of heat, high humidity, or diseases, do better in massed beds. Popular varieties grown from cuttings are 'Cherry Blossom', 'Glacier', 'Sincerity', 'Snowmass', 'Sunbelt', 'Veronica', and 'Yours Truly'. Popular varieties from seed are the 'Diamond' (AAS, FS), 'Elite', 'Hollywood' (FS, RHS), 'L'Amour', 'Orbit', 'Pinto', 'Ringo', 'Sprinter' (ABT, FS), and 'Video' (RHS) series, which are available in many colors, and 'Double Steady Red'.

The Martha Washington, Lady Washington, or Regal geranium, *P. domesticum*, has deeply lobed and serrated leaves and large flowers in the same color range as other geraniums but with dark blotches on the upper petals. Ivy geraniums, *P. peltatum*, are popular choices for hanging baskets and ground covers. Leaves are ivy shaped on 36in (90cm) stems. Flowers are similar in shape and color to zonal geraniums, but are in looser clusters. 'Cascade' and 'Summer Showers' (FS) are popular varieties.

■ **HOW TO GROW** Cutting geraniums are rooted in coarse sand. Seed geraniums are sown indoors 12 to 16 weeks before the last frost. Germination takes 5 to 15 days. Ivy geraniums are propagated by cuttings, and 'Summer Showers' is grown from seeds in the same way as zonal geraniums. Martha Washingtons are propagated by cuttings. Since viruses can be transmitted by cuttings, it is more desirable to purchase plants that have been commercially grown than to root your own, as professional growers can provide virus-free plants.

Space plants 8–12in (20–30cm) apart in rich, slightly acid, fertile, moist, well-drained soil. Zonal geraniums must be grown in full sun, and ivy and Martha Washington geraniums benefit from light shade. Martha Washingtons can be grown only in cool climates. Keep faded flowers cut to keep the plants neat and encourage further blooming. Geraniums can be dug or rooted in the autumn and grown indoors.

Pelargonium x hortorum 'HOLLYWOOD STAR'

Pelargonium domesticum 'DELILAH'

Perilla frutescens

PERILLA FRUTESCENS

BEEFSTEAK PLANT

TOOTHED, DEEP REDDISH purple leaves have a metallic bronzy sheen. Although the 18–36in (45–90cm) plant bears pale lavender, pink, or white flowers in late summer, it is primarily grown for its foliage. Use it in borders and designs where a colored foliage plant is needed. Varieties include 'Atropurpurea' and 'Crispa'.

■ **HOW TO GROW** Sow seeds outdoors after all danger of frost has passed, or start them inside four to six weeks earlier. Do not cover seeds as light is necessary during the 15- to 20-day germination. Transplant carefully as beefsteak plant does not like having its roots disturbed. Plant 12–15in (30–38cm) apart in full sun or light shade in average to dry, fertile soil with good drainage. Pinch when 6in (15cm) tall to induce bushiness. If allowed to bloom, it self-sows readily.

PETUNIA X HYBRIDA

PETUNIA

PETUNIAS HAVE A spreading or cascading habit and bloom in every color of the rainbow. Many are solid colored; others are splashed, starred, zoned, speckled, striped, veined, or picoteed (white margined). There are two basic classes of petunias. Multiflora petunias produce a great abundance of small blooms, while grandiflora types have fewer but larger flowers. Mutliflora petunias are also more disease-resistant. Both classes include single, trumpet-shaped varieties and double varieties. Petunias bloom superbly in beds, borders or containers on top of fuzzy leaves. Grandiflora singles include the 'Cascade' and 'Supercascade', 'Cloud', 'Daddy' (AAS), 'Falcon', 'Flash', 'Frost', 'Magic' and 'Supermagic', 'Picotee' (FS), 'Prio' (RHS), 'Sails' and 'Ultra' series. 'Appleblossom' (AAS), and

Petunia x hybrida 'ULTRA CRIMSON STAR' (AAS)

Petunia x hybrida 'RESISTO DWARF ROSE'

'Ultra Crimson Star' (AAS). Grandiflora doubles include 'Blue Danube' and 'Purple Pirouette' (AAS). Multiflora singles include the 'Carpet', 'Joy', 'Madness', 'Pearls', 'Plum', 'Polo' (AAS), and 'Resisto' series, 'Comanche', and 'Summer Sun'. The best-known multiflora double is the 'Tart' series.

■ **HOW TO GROW** Start seeds indoors 10 to 12 weeks before the last spring frost. Do not cover the fine seeds which need light to germinate; germination takes 10 days. Seeds of doubles and hybrids need extra warmth to germinate. Space plants 8–12in (20–30cm) apart in sun or light shade. Soil should be sandy, dry and well drained. Pinch at planting time to encourage bushiness and cut plants back if they become leggy.

PHLOX DRUMMONDII

PHLOX

ANNUAL PHLOX IS A compact, mounded plant growing 6–18in (15–45cm) tall. The flowers are round or star-shaped and flower in clusters. Colors include white, pink, blue, red, salmon, and lavender. Use phlox for edging, bedding, borders, rock gardens, and containers. Varieties include 'Brilliant', 'Dwarf Beauty' (RHS), 'Globe', 'Petticoat', and 'Twinkle'.

■ **HOW TO GROW** Seeds may be sown outdoors in spring as soon as the ground can be worked or started indoors in individual pots 10 weeks earlier. A cool room is critical for germination, which takes 10 to 15 days. Cover the seeds completely as they need darkness to germinate. Annual phlox is very prone to damping off. Plant in full sun, 6in (15cm) apart, in rich, light, fertile, moist, well-drained soil. Keep faded flowers removed; shearing the plants back will encourage compactness and further bloom. Phlox is fairly heat-tolerant although some decline in flowering may be seen in midsummer.

Phlox Drummondii 'PETTICOAT PINK'

Portulaca grandiflora

PORTULACA

MOSS ROSE, SUN PLANT

MOSS ROSE IS A vining, spreading, ground-hugging plant 4–6in (10–15cm) high that is best used as an edging, border, ground cover, or in containers. Most flowers close up at night, in shade or on cloudy days. The best-known moss rose is *P. grandiflora*, which has needlelike leaves and ruffled single or double flowers of pink, red, gold, yellow, cream, orange, white, or salmon. 'Calypso', 'Cloudbeater', 'Sundance', 'Sunny-boy', and 'Sunnyside' are common varieties. *P. oleracea*

'Giganthea', has double yellow flowers; 'Wildfire' is a good variety.

■ **HOW TO GROW** Sow seeds outdoors after all danger of frost has passed, or start them indoors 8 to 10 weeks earlier. Germination takes 10 to 15 days. Space plants 12–15in (30–38cm) apart in full sun and dry, infertile, well-drained soil. Moss rose withstands heat and drought. Flowers fall cleanly as they fade and plants self-sow easily.

PRIMULA

PRIMROSE

PRIMROSES ARE A large group of 12in (30cm) plants with large, oblong or heart-shaped textured leaves and bright flowers in many colors, some with interesting contrasts and markings. The single flowers bloom in clusters on top of leafless stems. While many primroses are perennials, others are annuals grown in containers, formal beds, borders, or shade gardens. *P. malacoides*, fairy primrose, has flowers of rose, lavender, or white in loose clusters. *P. obconica*, German primrose, has blooms of purple, pink, red, or white. Some people develop an allergic reaction to the foliage of this primrose. *P. X polyantha*, polyanthus, is a short-lived perennial that is grown as an annual, and has flowers of white, purple, blue, red, pink, or yellow, many with centers in a contrasting color.

■ **HOW TO GROW** Sow seeds outdoors in late fall or early spring, or start plants indoors up to six months before outdoor planting. Germination takes 21 to 40 days. Do not cover the fine seeds which need light to germinate. Space plants 8–10in (20–25cm) apart in part shade and rich, moist, fertile, cool, slightly acid, well-drained soil.

Primula x polyantha

Primula malacoides   'LOVELY ROSE'

Primula obconica   'APPLE BLOSSOM'

Rudbeckia hirta 'DOUBLE GOLD'

RUDBECKIA HIRTA
GLORIOSA DAISY

RELATED TO BLACK-EYED SUSANS, gloriosa daisies grow 8–36in (20–90cm) tall and have single or double flowers of gold, yellow, bronze, orange, brown, or mahogany, often zoned or banded, with brown, yellow, green, or black cone-shaped centers. Gloriosa daisies grow well in borders and wildflower gardens, and are good grown for cut flowers. Good varieties are 'Goldilocks' (FS), 'Irish Eyes', and 'Marmalade'.

■ **HOW TO GROW** Start seeds indoors six to eight weeks before the last frost. Germination takes 5 to 10 days. Space plants 12–24in (30–60cm) apart in full sun or light shade and in average garden soil. Gloriosa daisies are heat- and drought-tolerant. Cut flowers as they fade. They are susceptible to mildew; see Diseases, earlier.

SALPIGLOSSIS SINUATA
PAINTED TONGUE

PAINTED TONGUE HAS tubular, velvety, heavily veined or textured trumpet-shaped flowers of purple, red, yellow, blue, and rose. Plants grow 24–36in (60–90cm) tall; foliage and stems are slightly hairy. Use them in borders, as backgrounds, and grow them for cut flowers. 'Bolero', 'Emperor', 'Kew Blue', and 'Splash' are good varieties.

■ **HOW TO GROW** Seeds can be sown outdoors in midspring, several weeks before the last expected frost, or started indoors eight weeks earlier. Seeds are very fine and should not be covered. Since they also need darkness to germinate, cover the seed flats with black plastic until germination occurs in 15 to 20 days. Plant painted tongue in full sun, 8–12in (20–30cm) apart in rich, light, moist, alkaline soil with excellent drainage. Mulch to keep the soil cool. Painted tongue does best where summers are cool. Tall varieties may need to be staked.

Salpiglossis sinuata 'SPLASH'

Salvia splendens

SALVIA, SAGE

SALVIA IS USEFUL in massed plantings, beds, borders, containers, or grown for cut flowers. *S. splendens*, scarlet sage, has spikes of red, white, purple, blue, or salmon flowers over dark green, waxy leaves. Plants grow 6–24in (15–60cm) tall. Varieties include 'Bonfire', 'Carabiniere', 'Hotline', 'Red Hot Sally', 'Red Pillar', and 'St John's Fire'. *S. farinacea* has thin flower spikes of blue, violet, or white. Leaves are gray-green and the plant grows to 24in (60cm). 'Rhea' and 'Victoria' (FS) are popular varieties.

■ **HOW TO GROW** Start seeds of scarlet sage indoors 8 to 10 weeks before the last frost. Do not cover seeds of red-flowered varieties which need light during the 10- to 15-day germination period. *S. farinacea* needs to be started indoors 12 weeks before the last frost. Space plants 8–12in (20–30cm) apart in full sun or part shade and in rich, well-drained soil. Although salvia will tolerate dry soil, it grows better if evenly watered.

Salvia farinacea 'VICTORIA WHITE' (FS)

SANVITALIA PROCUMBENS

CREEPING ZINNIA

SMALL, OVAL, DARK GREEN leaves set off sprightly, single or double, daisylike blooms of yellow or orange with purple centers. Plants grow 4–8in (10–20cm) tall and spread 10–16in (25–40cm) wide. Creeping zinnia is a sturdy annual for borders, beds, edgings, containers, and hanging baskets, and is an excellent ground cover. Varieties include 'Gold Braid' and 'Mandarin Orange' (AAS).

■ **HOW TO GROW** Seeds may be sown outdors after all danger of frost has passed or started indoors in individual pots four to six weeks earlier. Seeds need light to germinate, which takes 10 to 15 days. Set plants 5–6in (12.5–15cm) apart in full sun and in light, open, well-drained soil. They tolerate drought. Flowers fall cleanly as they fade.

Sanvitalia procumbens 'MANDARIN ORANGE' (AAS)

DUSTY MILLER

SENECIO CINERARIA AND S. VIRA-VIRA

DUSTY MILLER

DUSTY MILLER is a common name given to a number of plants that have silver and/or gray, velvety, lobed or deeply cut foliage, and no significant flowers. They are grown exclusively for the leaves and are used as buffers between strong colors, as borders, or as edgings in gardens often enjoyed at night, when the gray foliage seems almost luminescent. Plants grow 8–24in (20–60cm) high. *S. Cineraria* is very similar to *S Vira-Vira*, with *S. Vira-Vira* having a looser habit. In addition

to these two species, *Centaurea cineraria* and *Chrysanthemum ptarmiciflorum* are also called dusty miller and are similar in appearance and care. 'Cirrhus', 'Silverdust', and 'Silver Lace' are common varieties.

■ **HOW TO GROW** Start seeds indoors 8 to 10 weeks before the last frost. Germination takes 10 to 14 days. Space plants 12in (30cm) apart in full sun or light shade. Soil should be light, sandy, dry, and well drained. If plants start to get leggy, they can be sheared back.

TAQETES

MARIGOLD

THE YELLOW, RED, GOLD, orange, and maroon tones of marigolds are at home in beds, borders, mass plantings, edgings, or containers, or can be grown for cut flowers. There are five basic types of marigolds. The tallest ones (*Taqetes erecta*), African marigolds, grow from 12–36in (30–90cm) tall and have very full, double or carnation-shaped flowers. Varieties include the 'Climax', 'Crush', 'Discovery', 'Galore' (AAS, RHS), 'Gold Coin', 'Inca', 'Jubilee', 'Lady' (AAS), 'Monarch', 'Perfection', and 'Voyager' series, and 'Toreador' (AAS, RHS). The shorter, earlier blooming French marigolds (*Taqetes patula*) grow 6–16in (15–40cm) tall and have a profusion of small single, crested, anemone or carnation-shaped flowers. Popular varieties are the 'Aurora', 'Bonanza', 'Boy', 'Disco' (FS), 'Espana' (FS), 'Hero', 'Jacket' (FS), 'Janie', 'Marietta' (AAS), 'Golden Gate' (AAS), 'Honeycomb' (FS), and 'Red Cherry'.

A cross between French and African marigolds, (*Taqetes patula X erecta*), is known as a triploid or a 'mule.' Because the flowers are sterile, they produce all summer, even when it is very hot and other marigolds lose their free-flowering habit. 'Mighty Marietta', the 'Nuggets', 'Red Seven Star', and 'Sundance' are good varieties. Plants grow to 18in (45cm) high.

Taqetes tenuifolia, Signet marigold, has fine, lacy, lemon-scented foliage, grows 12in (30cm) tall, and has tiny, single flowers. The 'Gem' series is best known. *Taqetes filifolia*, Irish Lace, has fine, fernlike foliage and insignificant white to slightly green flowers.

■ **HOW TO GROW** Start seeds indoors four to six weeks before the last frost. Germination takes five to seven days. Seeds of French marigolds can be sown outdoors after frost danger has passed. African marigolds are sensitive to day length and will not bloom until late summer unless they are planted in bud or in bloom. Space marigolds a distance apart equal to one-half their final height. Marigolds like full sun and average soil and are relatively heat-resistant. To encourage continuous bloom, except for triploids which do not set seed, pick off faded flowers on a regular basis.

Tagetes erecta 'DISCOVERY ORANGE'

Tagetes patula 'QUEEN MIX'

Thunberqia alata 'SUSIE'

THUNBERQIA ALATA

BLACK-EYED SUSAN VINE

VINES GROW 6ft (2m) high and have dense, dark green, arrowhead-shaped leaves. Flowers are bell-shaped and tubular, and white, yellow, or orange. Flowers bloom both in clear colors, and with black eyes. Use black-eyed Susan vine for a ground cover, trellis, hanging basket, or container. 'Susie' is the best known variety.

■ **HOW TO GROW** Sow seeds outdoors after all danger of frost has passed, or start them indoors six to eight weeks earlier. Germination takes 15 to 20 days. Plant in full sun or very light shade in light, rich, moist, well-drained soil. Space plants 6in (15cm) apart and provide a support if you wish them to climb. Pick faded flowers as they form to keep the plants trim and productive. Black-eyed Susan vine grows best with a long, moderate temperature growing season.

TITHONIA ROTUNDIFOLIA

MEXICAN SUNFLOWER

MEXICAN SUNFLOWER, EXCEPT FOR a dwarf variety, grows 4–6ft (1.3–2 m) tall and has large, daisylike flowers of orange-red or yellow. The leaves are large, gray, and velvety. Plant it as a background, hedge or in a cutting garden. 'Goldfinger' and 'Torch' are common varieties.

■ **HOW TO GROW** Start seeds indoors six to eight weeks before the last frost, or outdoors after frost danger has passed. Germination takes 5 to 10 days. Do not cover seeds as light appears to be beneficial for germination. Plants should be spaced 2–3ft (0.6–1m) apart in full sun and dry garden soil with good drainage. Mexican sunflower is very heat- and drought-resistant.

Tithonia rotundifolia

Torenia Fournieri 'CLOWN MIX' (AAS)

TORENIA FOURNIERI

WISHBONE FLOWER

BUSHY PLANTS GROW 8–12in (20–30cm) tall and are covered with small flowers that have light violet upper lips and dark purple lower lips. In the throat of the flower is a pair of stamens that looks like a wishbone. Wishbone flower is used as an edging, bedding plant, border plant, or in containers. 'Clown Mix' (AAS) is the best variety.

■ **HOW TO GROW** Start seeds indoors 10 to 12 weeks before the last frost; germination takes 15 to 20 days. Wishbone flower prefers part or full shade, and rich, moist, well-drained soil. Set plants 6–8in (15–20cm) apart.

TROPAEOLUM MAJUS

NASTURTIUM

NASTURTIUM PLANTS COME IN three basic forms: bushy, growing to 12in (30cm) ('Jewel', 'Whirleybird'); semitrailing, reaching 24in (60cm) ('Gleam'); and vining, growing to 9ft (3m) ('Climbing Mixed'). Plants have single, semidouble, or double funnel-shaped flowers in tones of red, yellow, and orange. Flowers usually droop downward and are characterized by a black spur. Some are fragrant. Nasturtium leaves are round and dull and often used in salads. Flower buds or unripened seeds are used as a substitute for capers. The flowers are edible and can be used as a colorful garnish. Nasturtium can be used as a bedding plant, in containers and hanging baskets, on a trellis, or to overhang a wall.

■ **HOW TO GROW** Start seeds outdoors after all danger of frost has passed. Space plants 8–12in (20–30cm) apart in full sun or light shade. Soil must be light, well drained, infertile, and poor. Nasturtium does best where temperature is cool and humidity is high. In warm climates, bush types grow better than vining types. Where vining types are grown, the vines will need to be tied to their supports.

Tropaeolum majus (vining form)

Tropaeolum majus

Verbena x hybrida

VERBENA X HYBRIDA

VERBENA

VERBENA CREATES A stunning show of color in red, white, violet, purple, blue, cream, rose, or pink. Flowers bloom in clusters on spreading or upright 8–24in (20–60cm) plants. Use verbena as an edging, bedding plant, ground cover, rock garden plant, in hanging baskets, or grow for cut flowers. Varieties include 'Ideal Florist', 'Romance', 'Sandy' (AAS, FS), 'Showtime' (FS), 'Sparkle', 'Springtime', 'Trinindad' (AAS), and 'Tropic' (FS, RHS).

■ **HOW TO GROW** Start seeds indoors 10 to 12 weeks before the last frost. Cover the seed flat with black plastic until germination occurs, which takes 20 to 25 days. Germination of verbena is usually low, so sow extra heavily. Refrigeration of seeds for seven days prior to sowing may help. Verbena is particularly prone to damping off, and to powdery mildew when grown in heavy soil in humid conditions; see Diseases, earlier.

Plant spreading types 12–15in (30–38cm) apart, and upright types 8–10in (20–25cm) apart. Select a spot in full sun with light, fertile, well-drained soil. Verbena is tolerant of heat, drought, and poor soil, but is slow to become established.

Verbena x hyrida 'NOVALIS DEEP BLUE'

VIOLA X WITTROCKIANA

PANSY

PANSIES HAVE DAINTY, flat, single flowers with five round petals. Blooms are red, white, blue, pink, bronze, yellow, purple, lavender, or orange. Some are solid colored; in others the lower three petals are a different color from the top two petals. Many times a contrasting color forms a blotch or facelike marking on the lower three petals. Plants grow 6–15in (15–38cm) tall. Pansies are used in massed plantings, edgings, rock gardens, containers, and for spot color.

Pansies are classified as multiflora or grandiflora types, with the multifloras having a greater number of smaller flowers that come into bloom earlier. Multiflora varieties include 'Crystal Bowl', 'Jolly Joker' (AAS), 'Spring Magic', 'Springtime', and 'Universal'; grandiflora types are 'Imperial', 'Majestic Giant' (AAS), 'Mammoth Giant', 'Roc', and 'Swiss Giant'.

■ **HOW TO GROW** Plants can be set into the garden in early to midspring, as soon as the ground can be worked. Start seeds indoors 14 weeks earlier. Cover the seeds completely as they need darkness to germinate, which takes 10 to 20 days. Seeds also respond to being placed in the refrigerator in a moist medium for several days before sowing.

Where winter temperatures do not drop below 20°F (−7°C), pansies can be fall planted and mulched over winter to bloom early the following spring. Pansies can also be overwintered in cold frames and transplanted in early spring.

Set pansies 6–8in (15–20cm) apart in moist, rich, fertile soil and select a situation that offers sun to part shade. Pansies grow best where nights are cool. Remove flowers as they fade and pinch plants if they become leggy.

Viola x Wittrockiana 'SPRING MAGIC'

Zinnia elegans 'WHIRLIGIG'

Zinnia Haageana 'OLD MEXICO' (AAS)

Zinnia angustifolia

Zinnia elegans 'ZENITH MIXED' (AAS)

ZINNIA ELEGANS

ZINNIA

ZINNIAS GROW FROM DWARF, 6in (15cm) plants to tall varieties almost 4ft (1.3m) high. Flowers range from tiny buttons to huge, cactus-shaped blooms in every color of the rainbow except true blue. Use zinnias for edgings, borders, beds, hedges, backgrounds, or grow for cut flowers or container plants. Low-growing varieties are 'Dasher' (FS), 'Fantastic' (AAS), 'Peter Pan' (ABT), 'Small World', 'Rose Pinwheel', and 'Thumbelina' (AAS). Medium-sized varieties are 'Border Beauty' (AAS), 'Lilliput', 'Pulcino', and 'Splendor' (AAS). Tall varieties include 'Cut and Come Again', 'Ruffles' (AAS, FS), 'State Fair', 'Sunshine' (AAS), and 'Zenith' (AAS). Closely related species are *Z. angustifolia* (formerly called *Z. linearis*), which has single flowers of golden orange with yellow stripes on 8–12in (20–30cm) plants. Mexican zinnia, *Z. Haageana*, grows 12–18in (30–45cm) high and has single or double flowers in tones of red, mahogany, yellow, and orange. Some blooms are solid colored, others are two toned. 'Old Mexico' (AAS) and 'Persian Carpet' (AAS) are popular varieties.

■ **HOW TO GROW** Seeds can be sown outdoors after all danger of frost has passed or started indoors four weeks earlier. Germination takes five to seven days. Zinnias should be planted a distance apart equal to one-half of their ultimate height. Do not crowd them as they need good air circulation to inhibit mildew, which can be a major problem; see Diseases, earlier. Zinnias like full sun and a rich, fertile, well-drained soil. They are tolerant of heat and drought.

94

DESCRIPTIVE AND CULTIVATION DATA CHART

Colour: Bl=blue; B=brown; Br=bronze; C=cream; G=gold; L=lavender; O=orange; P=pink; Pu=purple;
R=red; Ro=rose; S=salmon; V=violet; W=white; Y=yellow.
Sun: FSh= full shade; FSun= full sun; LSh= light shade.
Soil: A=average - moderately rich and well-drained; D=dry - dries quickly, even after a heavy raid; M=moist
but well-drained - constantly, evenly moist but never soggy; R=rich - rich, fertile and well-drained.

GENUS	COLOR	HEIGHT	SUN	SOIL	SPACING
Ageratum houstonianum	Bl/P/W	6-12in/15-30cm	FSun/LSh	R/M	6-8in/15-20cm
Alternanthera ficoidea	Foliage	6in/15cm	FSun	A	8-10in/20-25cm
Althaea rosea	Many except Bl	2-6ft/0.6m-1.8m	FSun/LSh	R/M	18-24in/46-60cm
Amaranthus	Foliage + R	2-5ft/0.6m-1.6m	FSun	A/D	18-24in/45-60cm
Ammobium alatum	W	3ft/90cm	FSun	R/M	15in/38cm
Anchusa capensis	Bl	9-18in/23-46cm	FSun	D	10-12in/25-30cm
Antirrhinum majus	All except trueBl	6-36in/15-90cm	FSun/LSh	R	6-15in/15-38cm
Arctotis stoechadifolia	B/Br/P/Pu/O/R/W/Y	10-12in/25-30cm	FSun	D	12in/30cm
Begonia x semperflorens-cultorum	P/R/Ro/W	6-12in/15-30cm	LSh	R	6-8in/15-20cm
Begonia x tuberhybrida	O/P/R/W/Y	12in/30cm	LSh/FSh	R/M	12in/30cm
Brachycome iberidifolia	Bl/R/Ro/V/W	9-18in/23-46cm	FSun	R/M	6in/15cm
Brassica oleracea	Foliage/P/PU/W	10-12in/25-30cm	FSun	R/M	12-15in/30-38cm
Browallia speciosa	Bl/Pu/W	8-18in/20-45cm	LSh	R/M	6-10in/15-25cm
Calendula officinalis	O/Y	8-36in/20-90cm	FSun/LSh	R/M	12-15in/30-38cm
Callistephus chinesis	Bl/L/P/Pu/R/W/Y	6-36in/15-90cm	FSun	R/M	6-15in/15-38cm
Capiscum annuum	W+fruitsC/O/Pu/R/W	4-12in/10-30cm	FSun/LSh	R/M	6-9in/15-23cm
Catharanthus roseus	P/Ro/W	3-10in/7.5-25cm	FSun/LSh	A	6-24in/15-60cm
Celosia cristata	C/G/O/P/R/Ro/S/Y	6-30in/15-75cm	FSun	R	6-18in/15-45cm
Centaurea cyanus	Bl/L/P/Ro/W	12-36in/30-90cm	FSun	R/D	6-24in/15-60cm
Cleome hasslerana	L/P/Ro/W	3-6ft/1-2m	FSun	A/D	2-3ft/0.6-1m
Coleus x hybridus	Foliage	6-36in/15-90cm	LSh/FSh	R/M	10-12in/25-30cm
Coreopsis tinctoria	P/Pu/R/Y	8-36in/20-90cm	FSun	D	8-12in/20-30cm

GENUS	COLOR	HEIGHT	SUN	SOIL	SPACING
Cosmos	G/L/O/P/R/W/Y	3-4ft/1-1.3m	FSun	D	9-24in/23-60cm
Dahlia	All except Bl	1-3ft/0.3-1m	FSun/LSh	R/M	8-24in/20-60cm
Dianthus	P/R/Ro/W	6-24in/15-60cm	FSun	R	6-12in/15-30cm
Gaillardia pulchella	Br/R/Y	10-24in/25-60cm	FSun	D	10-24in/25-60cm
Gazania rigens	C/G/O/P/R/Y	8-10in/20-25cm	FSun	D	8-10in/20-25cm
Gerbera jamesonii	L/O/P/R/S/W/Y	12in/30cm	FSun	M/R	12-15in/30-38cm
Gomphrena	L/O/P/Pu/Ro/W/Y	30in/75cm	FSun	D	10-15in/25-38cm
Helianthus annuus	Br/G/Pu/R	15in/38cm; 4-6ft/1.3-2m	FSun	D	2-4ft/0.6-1.3m
Helichrysum bracteatum	P/Pu/R/S/W/Y	12-30in/30-75cm	FSun	D	9-15in/23-38cm
Hibiscus moscheutos	P/R/W	18in-6ft/45cm-2m	FSun/LSh	R/M	18in-4ft/45cm-1.3m
Hunnemannia fumariifolia	Y	2ft/0.6m	FSun	D	9-12in/23-30cm
Iberis	L/P/R/Ro/W	8-20in/20-50cm	FSun	A	6-10in/15-25cm
Impatiens balsamina	L/P/Pu/R/S/W/Y	10-36in/ 25-90cm	FSun/LSh	R/M	6-15in/15-38cm
Impatiens ëNew Guineaí	L/O/P/Pu/R/S	12-24in/30-60cm	LSh/FSun	R/M	12in/30cm
Impatiens wallerana	O/P/R/S/V/W	18in/45cm	FSun/Fsh	R	10-18in/25-45cm
Ipomoea	Bl/P/Pu/R/W	10-30ft/3-9m	FSun	D	12-18in/30-45cm
Kochia scoparia forma trichophylla	Foliage/R	3ft/1m	FSun	D	18-24in/45-60cm
Lathyrus odoratus	Bl/P/Pu/R/Ro/W	6ft/2m or 2.5ft/0.75m	FSun	R/M	6-8in/15-20cm or 15in/38cm
Lavatera trimestris	P/R/W	2-3ft/0.6-1m	FSun	D	15-24in/38-60cm
Lobelia erinus	Bl/P/Pu/W	4in/10cm	FSun/LSh	R/M	8-10in/20-25cm
Lobularia maritima	L/Pu/R/W	3-4in/7.5-10cm	FSun/LSh	A	10-12in/25-30cm
Matthiola incana	Bl/C/P/Pu/R/Ro/W	12-18in/30-45cm	FSun	R/M	12-15in/30-38cm
Mimulus x hybridus	G/R/Y	6-10in/15-25cm	LSh/FSh	R/M	6in/15cm
Mirabilis jalapa	P/R/V/W/Y	18-36in/45-90cm	FSun	D	12-18in/30-45cm
Nemesia strumosa	Bl/Br/C/G/L/O/P/R/W/Y	8-18in/20-45cm	FSun/LSh	R/M	6in/15cm

GENUS	COLOR	HEIGHT	SUN	SOIL	SPACING
Nemophila menziesii	Bl	6in/15cm	LSh/FSun	D	8-12in/20-30cm
Nicotiana alata	P/Pu/R/W/Y	10-18in/25-45cm	FSun/LSh	R	10-12in/25-30cm
Nierembergia hippomanica	Bl/V	6-12in/15-30cm	FSun/LSh	M	6-9in/15-23cm
Nigella damascena	Bl/P/Pu/W	12-24in/30-60cm	FSun	M	8-10in/ 20-25cm
Papaver	O/P/Pu/R/W/Y	1ft/0.3m or 3ft/1m	FSun	R/D	9-12in/23-30cm
Pelargonium	L/P/R/Ro/S/W	8-24in/20-60cm	FSun/LSh	R/M	8-12in/20-30cm
Perilla frutescens	L/P/W	18-36in/45-90cm	FSun/LSh	A/D	12-15in/30-38cm
Petunia x hybrida		All	FSun/LSh	D	8-12in/20-30cm
Phlox drummondii	Bl/L/P/R/S/W	6-18in/15-45cm	FSun	R/M	6in/15cm
Portulaca	C/G/O/P/R/S/W/Y	4-6in/10-15cm	FSun	D	12 15in/30-38cm
Primula	Many	12in/30cm	LSh	R/M	8-10in/20-25cm
Rudbeckia hirta	B/Br/G/O/Y	8-36in/20-90cm	FSun/LSh	A	12-24in/30-60cm
Salpiglossis sinuata	Bl/Pu/R/Ro/Y	24-36in/60-90cm	FSun	R/M	8-12in/20-30cm
Salvia	Bl/Pu/R/S/W	6-24in/15-60cm	FSun/LSh	R	8-12in/20-30cm
Sanvitalia procumbens	O/Y	4-8in/10-20cm	FSun	D	5-6in/12.5-15cm
Senecio cineraria & S. vira-vira	Silver/grey foliage	8-24in/20-60cm	FSun/LSh	D	12in/30cm
Tagetes	G/O/R/Y	6-36in/15-90cm	FSun	A	3-18in/7.5-45cm
Thunbergia alata	O/W/Y	6ft/2m	FSun/LSh	R/M	6in/15cm
Tithonia rotundifolia	O/R/Y	4-6ft/1.3-2m	FSun	D	2-3ft/0.6-1m
Torenia fournieri	Pu/V	8-12in/20-30cm	LSh/FSh	R/M	6-8in/15-20cm
Tropaeolum majus	O/R/Y	12-24in/30-60cm or 9ft/3m	FSun/LSh	D	8-12in/20-30cm
Verbena x hybrida	Bl/C/P/Pu/R/Ro/V/W	8-24in/20-60cm	FSun	D	8-15in/20-38cm
Viola x wittrockiana	Bl/Br/L/O/P/ Pu/R/W/Y	6-15in/15-38cm	FSun/LSh	M/R	6-8in/15-20cm
Zinnia elegans	All except true Bl	6in-4ft/15cm-1.3m	FSun	R	3in-24in/ 7.5cm-60cm

Descriptive and Cultivation Data Chart

COLOUR: B=blue; L=lavender; O=orange; P=pink; Pu=purple; R=red; W=White; Y=yellow.
BLOOM: Sp=spring; ESp=early spring; Su=summer; ESu=early summer; A=autumn; EA=early autumn.
SUN: FSun=full sun; LSh=light shade; FSh=full shade.
SOIL: A= average- moderately rich and well-drained; D=dry-dries quickly, even after a heavy rain; M=moist but well-drained-constantly, evenly moist but never soggy.

GENUS	COLOR	HEIGHT	BLOOM	SUN	SOIL	SPACING
Achillea	P/R/W/Y	18in-4ft/45cm-1.2m	Su	FSun	A/D	10-18in/25-45cm
Aconitum	B/L/Pu	3-4ft/90cm-1.2m	Su/EA	FSun/LSh	M	18in/45cm
Adenophora	B	2-3ft/60-90cm	Su	FSun/LSh	M	12in/30cm
Alchemilla	Y	12-18in/30-45cm	Sp/ESu	FSun/LSh	M	12in/30cm
Amsonia	B	2-3ft/60-90cm	Sp/ESu	FSun/LSh	A/D	18in/45cm
Anaphalis	W	2ft/60cm	Su	FSun/LSh	M	12in/30cm
Anchusa	B	18in-4ft/45cm-1.2m	Sp/ESu	FSun/LSh	A	18-24in/45-60cm
Anemone	P/Pu/R/W	1-4ft/30cm-1.2m	Sp or A	FSun/LSh	A/M	8-18in/20-45cm
Anthemis	Y	10-24in/25-60cm	Su	FSun	A/D	12-15in/30-38cm
Aquilegia	B/P/R/W/Y/Pu	1-3ft/30-90cm	Sp/ESu	FSun/LSh	A	12in/30cm
Arabis	W/P	8in/20cm	Sp	FSun	A/D	8-12in/20-30cm
Armeria	R/P/W	6-18in/15-45cm	Sp/ESu	FSun	A/D	8-12in/20-30cm
Artemisia	Foliage/W	1-6ft/30cm-1.8m	Su	FSun	A/D	12-24in/30-60cm
Aruncus	W	1-5ft/30cm-1.5m	Su	LSh	M	24-30in/60-75cm
Asarum	Foliage	6in/15cm		LSh/FSh	M	8-12in/20-30cm
Asclepias	O	2-3ft/60-90cm	Su	FSun	A/D	12in/30cm
Aster	B/P/Pu/R/W	6in-6ft/15cm-1.8m	Su/A	FSun	M	12-18in/30-45cm
Astilbe	P/R/W	1-4ft/30cm-1.2m	Su	LSh	M	12-18in/30-45cm
Aubrietia	Pu/L/P/R	6in/15cm	Sp	FSun/LSh	D	6-8in/15-20cm
Aurinia/Alyssum	Y	12in/30cm	Sp	FSun	A/D	8-12in/20-30cm
Baptisia	B	3-4ft/90cm-1.2m	ESu	FSun/LSh	A	2ft/60cm
Belamcanda	O	12-30in/30-75cm	Su	FSun/LSh	A	12in/30cm
Bellis	P/R/W	3-6in/7.5-15cm	Sp/ESu	FSun/LSh	M	6in/15cm
Bergenia	P/R/W	12in/30cm	Sp	FSun/LSh	A/M	12in/30cm
Brunnera		12-18in/30-45cm	Sp	FSun/LSh	M	12in/30cm
Campanula	B/W/P/Pu	6in-5ft/15cm-1.5m	Su/A	FSun/LSh	A/M	10-24in/25-60cm
Centaurea	B/Pu/Y/W/P	2-4ft/60cm-1.2m	Sp/Su	FSun	A	18in/45cm
Centranthus	R/P/W	3ft/90cm	Su	FSun/LSh	A	12-18in/30-45cm
Cerastium	W	6in/15cm	ESu	FSun	A/D	12in/30cm
Chrysanthemum	L/O/P/Pu/R/W/Y	1-4ft/30cm-1.2m	LSu/A	FSun	A	12-18in/30-45cm

GENUS	COLOR	HEIGHT	BLOOM	SUN	SOIL	SPACING
Chrysogonum	Y	4-6in/10-15cm	Sp/ESu	LSh/FSh	M	12in/30cm
Cimicifuga	W	2-8ft/60cm-2.4m	Su	FSun/FSh	M	2ft/60cm
Clematis	B/L/W	2-5ft/60cm-1.5m	Su	FSun/LSh	M	18in/45cm
Coreopsis	Y	6-30in/15-75cm	Su/A	FSun	A	12in/30cm
Delphinium	B/L/P/Pu/W	1-6ft/30cm-1.8m	Su	FSun/LSh	m	12-30in/30-75cm
Dianthus	P/R/W	6-18in/15-45cm	Sp/Su	FSun	A/D	8-12in/20-30cm
Dicentra	R/P/W	10-36in/25-90cm	Sp/Su	LSh/FSh	M	1-2ft/30-60cm
Dictamnus	W/P	2-3ft/60-90cm	ESu	FSun/LSh	M	3ft/90cm
Digitalis	P/R/W/Y	1-4ft/30cm-1.2m	ESu	FSun/LSh	M	12-16in/30-40cm
Doronicum	Y	12-30in/30-75cm	Sp/ESu	FSun/LSh	M	12in/30cm
Echinacea	P/W	2-4ft/60cm-1.2m	Su/A	FSun/LSh	A/D	18in/45cm
Echinops	B	3-5ft/90cm-1.5m	Su	FSun	A/D	18-24in/45-60cm
Erigeron	B/P/W/L	18-30in/45-75cm	Su	FSun/LSh	D	12in/30cm
Eryngium	B/W/L	1-4ft/30cm-1.2m	Su	FSun	D	1-2ft/30-60cm
Eupatorium	B/P	2-10ft/60cm-3m	Su/A	FSun	A/M	18-36in/45-90cm
Euphorbia	Y/R/W	6-36in/15-90cm	Sp/Su	FSun	D	12-18in/30-45cm
Ferns	Foliage	6in-6ft/15cm-l.Sm		LSh/FSh	A/M	12-30in/30-75cm
Filipendula	P/W	18in-7ft/45cm-2.lm	Sp/Su	FSun/LSh	A/M	1-2ft/30-60cm
Gaillardia	O/R/Y	12-30in/30-75cm	Su/A	FSun	A/D	6-18in/ 15-45cm
Galium	Foliage/W	6-8in / 15-20cm	Sp	LSh	M	12in/30cm
Geranium	L/P/Pu/W	6-24in / 15-30cm	Sp/Su	FSun	A	12in/30cm
Geum	R/Y/O	1-2ft/30-60cm	Su	FSun/LSh	M	12-18in/30-45cm
Gypsophila	W/P	4in-3ft/10-90cm	Su	FSun	A	1-2ft/30-60cm
Helenium	R/Y/O	2-6ft/60cm-1.8m	Su/A	FSun	M	18-24in/45-60cm
Heliopsis	Y	2-6ft/60cm-1.8m	Su/A	FSun	A/M	2ft/60cm
Helleborus	W/P/pu	1-2ft/30-60cm	ESp	FSun/LSh	M	18in/45cm
Hemerocallis	Y/O/P/R/Pu	1-6ft/30cm-l.8m	Su/A	FSun/LSh	A/M	1-2ft/30-60cm
Hesperis	P/Pu/W	2-3ft/60-90cm	Sp/ESu	FSun/LSh	M	18in/45cm
Heuchera	R/P/W	1-2ft/30-60cm	Su/A	FSun/LSh	M	12in/30cm
Hibiscus	R/P/W	2-8ft/60cm-2.4m.	Su/A	FSun	M	3ft/90ern
Hosta	Pu/L/W/Foliage	6in-3ft/ 15-90cm	Su/A	LSh/FSh	M	1-2ft/30-60cm
Iberis	W	6-10in/15-25cm	Sp	FSun	M	15in/38cm
Iris	All colours	6in-4ft/15cm-1.2m	Sp/Su	FSun/LSh	A/M	12-18in/30-45cm
Kniphofia	O/R/Y	1-4ft/30cm-1.2m	Su	FSun	M	18in/45cm
Lavandula	L/Pu/P/W	1-3ft/30-90cm	Su	FSun	A/D	12in/30cm

GENUS	COLOR	HEIGHT	BLOOM	SUN	SOIL	SPACING
Liatris	P/Pu/W	18in-5ft/45cm-1.5m	Su/A	FSun	A/M	12-18in/30-45cm
Linum	B/W/Y	1-2ft/30-60cm	Su	FSun	A/M	18in/45cm
Lobelia	R/B/Pu	2-4ft/60cm-1.2m	Su/A	LSh	M	12-18in/30-45cm
Lupinus	B/P/Pu/R/W/Y	2-3ft/60-90cm	ESu	FSun/LSh	M	18-24in/45-60cm
Lychnis	O/Pu/W/R	1-3ft/30-90cm	Su	FSun	A	12in/30cm
Lysimachia	W/Y	18-36in/45-90cm	Su	FSun/LSh	M	18-24in/45-60cm
Lythrum	P/Pu	30in-4ft/75cm-1.2m	Su/A	FSun	M	18in/45cm
Macleaya	W	6-10ft/1.8-3m	Su	FSun	A	3-4ft/90cm-1.20m
Marrubium	W	2-3ft/60-90cm	Su	FSun	A/D	12in/30cm
Mertensia	B/P/W	1-2ft/30-60cm	Sp	LSh	M	8-12in/20-30cm
Monarda	P/Pu/R/W	2-4ft/60cm-1.2m	Su	FSun/LSh	A/M	18in/45cm
Nepeta	B/W	12-18in/30-45cm	Sp/ESu	FSun	A/D	12-18in/30-45cm
Oenothera	Y/P	1-2ft/30-60cm	Su	FSun	A	18in/45cm
Orn. Grasses	Tan/W/Foliage	8in-6ft/20cm-l.8m	Su/A	FSun/LSh	A/M	1-2ft/30-9 0cm
Paeonia	P/R/W	2-3ft/60-90cm	LSp/ESu	FSun	M	2-3ft/60-90cm
Papaver	O/R/P/W	2-4ft/60cm-1.2m	ESu	FSun	A	18in/45cm
Phlox	P/Pu/R/W/B	6in-4ft/15cm-1.2m	Sp/A	FSun/LSh	M	1-2ft/30-60cm
Physostegia	P/L/W	2-4ft/60cm-1.2m	Su/A	FSun	A/M	18-24in/45-60cm
Platycodon	B/P/W	18-30in/45-75cm	Su	FSun/LSh	A/D	12-18in/30-45cm
Polygonatum	W	1-6ft/30cm-l.8m	Sp	LSh/FSh	M	18-24in/45-60cm
Primula	B/L/Pu/R/W/Y	6-24in/15-60cm	Sp/ESu	LSh	M	12in/30cm
Pulmonaria	B/P/W	6-18in/15-45cm	Sp	LSh	M	12in/30cm
Rudbeckia	Y	2-6ft/60cm-1.8m	Su/A	FSun	A/M	18in/45cm
Salvia	B/Pu/P	18-36in/45-90cm	Su	FSun	A	12-18in/30-45cm
Scabiosa	B/L/W	1-2ft/30-60cm	Su/A	FSun	A/D	12in/30cm
Sedum	P/R/W/Y	4-24in / 10-60cm	Su/A	FSun	A/D	1-2ft/30-60cm
Smilacina	W	18-36in/45-90cm	Sp	LSh/FSh	M	12-18in/30-45cm
Solidago	Y	18-42in/45cm-1.05m	Su/A	FSun	A/D	18in/45cm
Stachys	Foliage/L/P/Pu	8-24in/20-60cm	Su	FSun/LSh	A/D	12in/30cm
Stokesia	B/W	1-2ft/30-60cm	Su/A	FSun	A	12-18in/30-45cm
Thalictrum	L/P/Y	3-5ft/90cm-1.5m	Sp/Su	FSun/LSh	M	18-24in/45-60cm
Thermopsis	Y	3-5ft/90cm-1.5m	ESu	FSun	A/D	2-3ft/60-90cm
Tradescantia	B/P/Pu/R/W	24-30in/60-75cm	Su	FSun/LSh	A/D	18in/45cm
Veronica	B/P/Pu/R/W	6-24in/15-60cm	Su	FSun	A	12-18in/30-45cm
Viola	B/Pu/0/R/W/Y	6-12in / 15-30cm	Sp/A	FSun/FSh	A/M	12in/30cm

HOW TO PLANT AND GROW
Perennials

Maggie Oster

INTRODUCTION

BILLOWING CLOUDS OF baby's breath, robust delphiniums reaching for the sky, translucent petals of poppies shimmering in the sun. These are a few of the images evoked by perennials in the garden. Perennials have provided generations of gardeners with a wealth of colors, shapes, textures, and sizes of plants and flowers, with bloom spanning the seasons from hellebores pushing through snow in winter to the hardiest of the chrysanthemums persisting well into the chilly days of fall. With thousands of different perennial varieties available, the hardest part is narrowing the choices.

What exactly is a perennial? Basically, it is a plant that lives more than two years. As that description would also include trees and shrubs, the word is further defined as being a plant that is herbaceous, or having soft, fleshy stems that die back to the ground in the fall. There are a few exceptions to this, such as many of the ornamental grasses, semi-woody sub-shrubs, and plants with evergreen foliage. While the foliage of most perennials dies each year, the roots are able to survive varying degrees of winter cold and send up new growth in the spring. A perennial may be able to do this for several years or for decades, depending on many factors.

Besides true perennials, certain biennial plants are included in this book. Biennials take two years to complete their life cycle: in the first year from seed they produce only leaves, and in the second they grow and bloom, set seed, and die.

USING PERENNIALS IN THE GARDEN

The most traditional way to use perennials is in borders, with the plants placed either in ribbonlike bands or in natural clumps. Except in very formal, geometric gardens, the latter method is generally preferred. Often, two parallel borders are developed, separated by a lawn, a walk, or both. A fence, hedge, or wall is often included as a backdrop. Free-standing beds, either in geometric shapes or in less formal undulating designs, are another way to use perennials in the landscape. Such beds are intended to be viewed from all sides.

The wealth of perennials available from around the world is also useful in many other ways in the landscape. A group of trees underplanted with a variety of ferns and other shade-loving perennials becomes a woodland garden. Perennials native to alpine areas or regions with

LEFT: *Free-standing beds are to be viewed from all sides and may be surrounded by lawn or paving. They may act as a divider or draw the garden visitor from one part of the garden to another.*

OPPOSITE ABOVE: *A meadow-like garden using ornamental grasses, day lilies, yarrow, geum, veronica, and black-eyed Susans turns this large expanse of lawn into a low-maintenance area.*

OPPOSITE BELOW: *Learning to combine plants successfully for a beautiful effect, such as this border of chrysanthemum, Japanese anemone, artemisia, liriope, physostegia, goldenrod, asters, and other plants, means taking the time to study, plan, and carefully choose.*

dry, gravelly soil are the best ones to choose in softening the harsh lines of a stone wall or making a rocky outcropping into a rock garden. A wet, marshy area along a stream or pool turns into a bog garden when planted with perennials that tolerate very moist conditions. An open expanse of lawn is transformed into a glorious meadow garden when filled with brightly

colored flowers and ornamental grasses that thrive in these conditions.

Perennials can also provide an accent in the landscape, or, when planted in containers, turn a deck or patio into a flower-filled retreat.

CONSIDERING GROWING CONDITIONS

As you begin the process of deciding what perennials you want to grow, first consider your growing conditions. These factors include minimum winter temperatures, soil, light, and water.

Hardiness is mainly determined by the ability of a plant to survive a minimum winter temperature. Water and soil conditions plus other factors also play a role. These work together so that even within a small yard there will be such microclimatic differences that a plant may survive in one corner but not in another. For example, temperatures will be lower at the bottom of a

one that gets morning sun and afternoon shade is usually the best option.

Heavily dappled shade under trees, the dense shade on the north side of a building, hedge, or fence, or any position with four hours or less of sun each day is considered full shade. Very few perennials bloom well in these conditions, but there are a number with beautiful foliage suitable for these areas.

For most perennials, the ideal soil, called loam, has a balanced mixture of sand, silt, and clay particles, drains well, and has a generous supply of organic matter, or humus. Fortunately, organic matter can make either sandy soil that drains too quickly or clay soil that drains slowly quite amenable, because it helps to retain water and nutrients while at the same time allowing air spaces around the plant roots. An additional benefit is that it enhances the growth of soil microorganisms that release plant nutrients. The most common sources of organic matter are peat moss, compost, or leaf mold.

To determine your soil type quickly, dig up a handful of soil three to five days after a rainfall and squeeze. If it forms a ball that does not readily break apart it is probably high in clay; a loose gritty soil is mainly sand, while a soil ball that crumbles loosely is a loam. To determine drainage, dig a hole 12 in (30 cm) deep and fill with water. If the water has not seeped away in an hour, the drainage is poor. If the poor drainage is due to a clay soil, adding organic matter is usually enough,

hill, on the north side of a house, or in an area exposed to wind. Good drainage is a key element, for should water be allowed to collect around roots and then freeze, the results are usually fatal. With experience, you will learn which areas are best for certain plants. You may even be able to find that extra warm spot for growing a plant that is not normally hardy in your area.

Although some perennials must have full sun, there are a great number that tolerate either full sun or light shade, plus others that grow best in light or even full shade. In regions with hot, humid summers, light or partial shade is often necessary for plants to survive. This may be provided by planting on the east or west side of a building, hedge, or fence so that sun is received for at least four to six hours each day. The lightly dappled shade beneath open trees is similar; this can be created by thinning out upper branches or trimming off lower ones. When choosing a lightly shaded site,

ABOVE LEFT: *With experience you will discover that different features of your yard will have climatic variations. A bed next to a stone wall that faces south or east will be hotter in both summer and winter than other parts of the yard because of the retained and reflected heat. Such an area would be good for heat-tolerant, marginally hardy plants.*

LEFT: *For garden with an abundance of shade there are perennial flowers and plants that will turn a dull area into one with a wealth of texture and form. A garden such as this one, planted with hostas, illustrates the many shade of green that foliage plants offer.*

but if it is due to other factors such as a hardpan, or impervious layer, beneath the top soil, then growing plants in raised beds or containers or installing drainage tiles should be considered.

Most plants grow best with an average of 1 in (2.5 cm) of rainfall or irrigation each week during the growing season. In choosing which plants to grow in your garden, consider either the natural rainfall or your willingness to supplement it. The use of a mulch helps to conserve soil moisture.

For most people, choosing plants with low-maintenance qualities is of prime importance. Some plants must be staked, others need to be divided frequently, pinched back, have faded flowers removed, be sprayed for pests, or other time-consuming chores.

DEVELOPING A DESIGN

Once you have established your growing conditions and considered the possible perennials, you are ready to develop a design. Borders are usually best if at least 4 ft (1.20 m) wide and beds at least 6 ft (1.80 m) at their widest. If there is a hedge behind a border, provide 2 ft (60 cm) of space between. A border is intended to be viewed from one, two or three sides, so place taller plants at the back with progressively shorter ones toward the front. With free-standing beds, place the tallest plants in the middle with plants of gradually decreas-

TOP: *An area shaded in the afternoon provides the ideal growing conditions for plants intolerant of heat or those that need light shade, such as this planting of hostas, astilbes, Solomon's seal, and ferns.*

ABOVE: *A quick way of determining your soil type is to pick up a handful, squeeze, then poke the soil ball with your fingers. If it crumbles easily, then you probably have the best – a loam soil.*

LEFT: *In designing a perennial border, place the taller flowers near the back, with progressively shorter flowers toward the front. Mixing in a few taller plants near the front gives the border a more dynamic look.*

ing heights toward the outer edges. Breaking this guideline occasionally helps to prevent monotony, and a group of tall plants in the front of a bed or border has a bold, dynamic effect. Placing some of the low-growing, spring-blooming plants toward the center of a bed or border makes it more interesting, too.

The season of bloom and growth habit of the plants are also to be considered. Some people may be satisfied with a perennial garden that is in bloom for a specific time of the year, while others want one border to be flowering as much of the growing season as possible.

Studying the plant descriptions, and the plant chart at the back of the book, as well as observing when these plants flower in your area, will help you to coordinate and combine the plants in your garden. Generally, using smaller plants in a compact garden and larger plants in a bigger garden is recommended; this guideline is best broken when a large, strongly architectural plant is used in a small garden for a dramatic accent.

In developing flower beds and borders, do not limit yourself strictly to perennials. Combining bulbs, annuals, herbs, and shrubs within a strong framework

OPPOSITE: *One of the goals in designing with perennials is to get as many months of beauty as possible. This front yard planted with masses of 'Autumn Joy' sedum, ornamental grasses, black-eyed Susan, and Russian sage provides an attractive landscape from midsummer well into winter.*

RIGHT: *Although perennials are quite wonderful enough to be used by themselves, they also combine well with other plants, including roses, shrubs, annuals, bulbs, and herbs.*

BELOW: *Monochromatic color schemes, using shades and tints of a single color, or analogous schemes, using adjoining colors, are calm and soothing. An example of a monochromatic scheme is black-eyed Susan planted with blackberry lily.*

of perennials will provide greater possibilities for color, form, and texture and a longer blooming season, plus more interest in the winter months.

A beautiful, aesthetically pleasing perennial garden utilizes basic artistic design principles with regard to color, texture, and form of flowers and foliage.

Studying a color wheel is helpful in combining colors. Basically, remember that reds, oranges, and yellows are warm colors and greens, blue, and violets are cool colors, with the former implying feelings of excitement and passion and the latter tranquility and calm. Cool colors tend to appear farther away from the viewer, while warm colors appear closer. This effect can be used to create illusions. Cool colors planted at the back of the garden make it seem larger, while a border of warm-colored flowers makes it seem smaller. Unfortunately, since cool colors recede, they tend to lose their impact far away and are best observed close-up. In combining warm and cool colors, warm colors are best used more sparingly as they can easily overwhelm the cooler-colored flowers.

In developing color schemes, it is helpful to understand that a pure color is called a hue, a tint is lighter, and a shade is darker. There are four basic color schemes. Monochromatic schemes utilize flowers in various tints and shades of one color. In a garden, green is always present, so a truly monochromatic garden is not possible. Analogous schemes usually utilize the tints and shades of three adjoining colors on the color wheel, such as yellow, yellow-orange and orange. Complementary schemes combine colors that are opposite on the color wheel, such as orange and blue or yellow and violet. These are difficult to achieve successfully, but by using pure hues, including white flowers or foliage, and intermingling plants, they can be very powerful.

LEFT: *Complementary color schemes utilize colors opposite on the color wheel, with the most popular combination being purple and yellow, such as this bed or catmint, yarrow, mountain bluet, and pinks.*

OPPOSITE: *Polychromatic color schemes, utilizing all the colors available, is a challenge to do well.*

BELOW: *Plant form and texture are two other important considerations beside color when designing with perennials. Repeating these is one way to strengthen the garden design. The open, spreading 'Ruby Glow' and 'Autumn Joy' sedums with medium-textured foliage is offset by the spiky, fine-textured blue fescue and coarser-textured yucca.*

Polychromatic schemes combine any and every colour; the result can be garish or pleasing.

Plant form is another important design consideration. The five basic forms of perennials are rounded, vertical, open, upright and spreading, and prostrate. Beds and borders may be composed of only one form, the repetition of several forms, combinations of complementary forms, or a mixture of all the forms.

Texture refers to the appearance of the plant, not to actually how it feels to the touch. The terms fine, medium, and coarse are determined by the size and density of the foliage and flowers. As with color, spatial illusions can be created with texture. Plants with coarse texture appear closer, and fine-textured ones seem further away. Coarse-textured plants at the back of the garden make the garden seem smaller, and fine-textured ones in a narrow border make it appear wider.

Once you have analyzed your site, considered the design basics, and made a list of plants you want to include, you are ready to draw a garden plan. Drawing a plan to scale on graph paper will help you to get a sense of the space and proportions as well as the number of plants needed. Determine the dimensions of the site and outline the shape of the bed or border on the graph paper. From your list of plants, begin drawing in the clumps of plants on a sheet of tracing paper laid over the graph paper; include as many of the plant characteristics, usually in code, as needed to help you to have an

ABOVE: *Many perennials are long-lived, so it is important to prepare the soil well. Remove rocks and compost the sod. With a spade, fork, or rototiller, work the soil at least 8 in (20 cm) deep, then incorporate a layer of organic matter and the recommended amount of fertilizer.*

accurate picture of the garden. For example, you might want information about height, form, color, and season of bloom. Overlaying layers of tracing paper can help in experimenting with different combinations or seeing how the garden will look at different seasons. Use colored pencils or markers to indicate colors, if desired. Unless the garden is very small, placing at least three of the same plants together gives the greatest impact.

Although this process may seem tedious, by carefully choosing plants suited for your area, your garden, and your preferences rather than just buying at random will give you a much better chance of having a breathtaking garden for many years to come.

PREPARING THE SOIL

Since the perennial garden is intended to bring lasting pleasure, adequate preparation of the soil before planting is worth every bit of effort. If the area is large or you are unfamiliar with the pH and nutrient levels in your yard, have the soil tested at a laboratory or use one of the simple soil test kits that are available from garden centers.

Soil can be damaged by digging when it is too wet, so wait until it is partially dry. Remove any large stones and compost the sod. For best results, use a spade or fork to turn the soil over to a depth of 12–18 in (30–45 cm); alternatively, rototill the soil as deeply as possible. Spread a 2–3-in (5–7.5-cm) layer of organic matter evenly on top. Sprinkle on lime to adjust pH, according to soil test recommendations, and granular or timed-release fertilizer, again according to test recommendations or directions on the package label. An average recommendation is 3–5 pounds (2.5–2.25 kg) of 5–10–5 or 5–10–10 fertilizer or 10 pounds (4.5 kg) of commercially dried cow or sheep manure per 100 square ft (9

RIGHT: *Perennials bought locally at a garden center or nursery may be growing in 4-inch (10-cm) or larger pots. Choosing plants locally allows you to see first-hand the quality and appearance of the plants.*

sq m). Using a spade or rototiller, work these ingredients into the soil. Rake the surface smooth.

BUYING AND PLANTING PERENNIALS

Perennial plants may be purchased locally at garden centers and nurseries, usually in 4-in (10-cm) or 1-gallon (3.75-litre) pots. Most of these plants will be old enough to bloom the first year. Select plants that are bushy and compact, with healthy green foliage and no sign of insects or diseases.

There is a great number of mail-order companies offering seed, while others ship young seedling plants, dormant bare-root plants, or older, larger plants in pots. Some companies are specialists in rare and unusual varieties. Many have colorful catalogs filled with detailed facts about the different plants, providing a valuable source of information. Most companies are reliable, but if you have never ordered by mail before, talk with other gardeners in your area to learn about their experiences. Spring catalogs are mailed in the middle of winter. Plants ordered then will be shipped in early spring as dormant bare-root plants, or later in containers.

If possible, plant on a day that is cool and cloudy, with rain predicted in a day or so. Planting in late afternoon is better than in the morning. Avoid hot or windy weather.

When planting dormant bare-root perennials, the roots should not dry out, so place small stakes at the proper spacings in the prepared soil, and unwrap and plant each one individually. With a trowel dig a hole large enough so the roots spread out. Except as noted in the Encyclopedia Section, set the point where the roots meet the stem or crown at ground level. Fill in with soil around the roots and tamp gently. Then water thoroughly.

Although container-grown plants can be planted at any time they are purchased during the growing season, planting in spring after the last frost is preferred. Rather than using stakes to mark planting spots, you can set the pots out and move them around until satisfied. When ready to plant, dig a hole, gently remove the plant from the pot, loosen the roots slightly with your fingers or cut them with a knife if they are very thick, and set into the hole. The soil level should be just slightly higher than in the pot, as the plant will settle. Then water thoroughly.

ABOVE: *Plants growing in containers can be planted almost any time during the growing season. Prepare the soil and dig a hole large enough for the roots to easily spread out. Gently remove the plant from the pot, loosen the roots, and set the plant in the hole at the same depth as in the pot. Fill in with soil around the roots, tamp gently, and water well.*

FERTILIZING

A complete fertilizer contains nitrogen, phosphorus, and potassium. The percentage of these elements, always in the order above, is described by the three numbers on the package, such as 5–10–10. Most perennials grown for their blooms do best with a fertilizer lower in nitrogen than the other two elements, as nitrogen benefits foliage growth at the expense of flowers. Fertilizer may be applied in granular form, timed-release pellets, or as a liquid.

Additional fertilizer is not necessary in the first year of planting if the area is well-prepared, although a light feeding in midsummer would be all right. In subsequent years, feed once in the spring with about 2 pounds (1 kg) of 5–10–10 or 5–10–5 per 100 square ft (9 sq m) and again in midsummer. Liquid fertilizers are especially good for spot feeding those plants that are heavy feeders or those that seem to need an extra boost.

ABOVE *Mulching with a several-inch (centimetre) layer of organic material, such as this partially composted ground bark and tree limbs, is beneficial in several ways. It helps the soil to retain moisture for longer, reduces the need for watering, deters weeds, keeps the soil cool, and adds vital organic material to the soil.*

WATERING

Although most perennials tolerate average soil, or one that briefly dries out, a great many perennials thrive in a soil that remains evenly moist but is never soggy. If natural rainfall does not provide this, supplemental watering is necessary.

The best method is to use a rubber, plastic, or canvas soaker hose laid among the plants. Water in the morning so the foliage has a chance to dry off before nightfall, as dampness encourages the spread of disease organisms. Soak the soil thoroughly; it should be moist 3–4 in (7.5–10 cm) deep.

WEEDING AND MULCHING

Weeds are inevitable in any garden. Try to pull them while they are still young before they get deep roots or flower and set seed. Try not to disturb the roots of the perennials. If a large clump of soil is removed when weeding, bring in additional topsoil from another part of the garden.

Adding a layer of organic mulch helps to keep weeds in check. It also slows down the evaporation of moisture from the soil, keeps the soil cool, which encourages root growth, and adds humus to the soil as it decomposes. In spring after removing any weeds, apply a layer of mulch several inches (cm) thick over the surface

of beds and borders, tapering it thinly near the perennials. Some of the possible organic mulches include buckwheat hulls, shredded hardwood or redwood bark, ground corncobs or leaves, rotted manure, or half-rotted compost.

STAKING

There are two types of staking needs: for the tall, single-stalked plants, such as delphinium, digitalis, and monkshood, and for plants with thin, floppy stems, such as yarrow, aster, chrysanthemum, and coreopsis.

Use bamboo stakes or wooden poles for the tall plants, inserting each one 12 in (30 cm) into the ground and 1 in (2.5 cm) from the stalk. Use a plant tie or twine to attach the stalk to the stake loosely. If the tie is too tight, the plant will be injured.

Bushy, thin-stemmed plants can be staked with any of several types of purchased supports or by encircling the plant with twiggy tree branches 18–24 in (45–60

ABOVE: *Stake single-stemmed tall plants, such as delphinium, with bamboo, wood, or metal stakes set 1 ft (30 cm) deep and tied loosely to the plant at several points along the stem.*

ABOVE: *Plants with many thin stems can be supported by surrounding the plants with twiggy tree branches in spring.*

cm) long. When the plant is half that height, insert several branches into the soil around the plant. As the season progresses, the foliage will hide the twigs.

PINCHING, THINNING, AND DISBUDDING

Pinching out the growing tip from a plant forces side branches to grow more readily, making plants shorter, sturdier, bushier, and with more flowers. Use your fingers to remove a small amount of the growth. This is usually done several times before the beginning of July. Chrysanthemums need this treatment but other perennials such as phlox and asters benefit as well.

Some perennials including phlox, delphinium, sneezeweed, shasta daisies, and asters, produce so many shoots that growth is spindly and air circulation is poor, which promotes fungus diseases. Thinning out some of the stalks when growth is 4–6 in (10–15 cm) tall will reduce this problem.

Disbudding, or removing some of the flower buds, allows the remaining bud to produce an extra large flower. Remove the small side buds early in development, if desired, on such plants as peonies, hibiscus, and large-flowered chrysanthemums.

DEADHEADING

A relatively self-explanatory term, deadheading refers to cutting off the dead, or faded, flowers. This not only makes the garden neater and cleaner, but also prevents seed development. This is often desirable because seed development can weaken the plant, cause it to stop blooming, or allow it to re-seed and become a nuisance. Often, the seedlings are of inferior quality to the parent, especially if the latter is a hybrid or other cultivar. With some early-blooming plants, such as lupine, phlox, anthemis, and delphinium, removing the faded flowers makes the plants bloom again in late summer or fall.

FALL CLEANUP AND WINTER PROTECTION

After several frosts have killed back plants, cut off the dead stems to 2–4 in (5–10 cm). Removing this debris

ABOVE: *Removing faded flowers and spent stems keeps the garden looking attractive, often encourages reblooming, and reduces the places pests can overwinter. Foliage and stems that are not diseased can be composted, which can then be used to enrich the soil or serve as a mulch.*

from the garden not only makes it look more attractive during the winter, but it also reduces the places where pests can overwinter.

A winter mulch protects tender plants and prevents shallow-rooted perennials from being heaved out of the ground through alternate freezing and thawing of the soil. To apply, wait until the ground has frozen to a depth of 2 in (5 cm) and plants are completely dormant. Then, spread a 3–6-in (7.5–1.5-cm) layer of loose, open mulch, such as oak leaves, salt hay, pine boughs, or ·straw around plants. This layer can be thicker for extra-tender perennials.

CONTROLLING PESTS AND DISEASES

Pests seldom become a serious problem with the great majority of perennials, especially if preventative measures are taken. These include:

- fertilizing and watering regularly so plants are vigorous and healthy and not stressed;
- growing varieties that are resistant to pests;
- picking off bugs and dropping them into a can of kerosene;
- using natural controls such as birds, toads, ladybugs, praying mantis, and other animals that eat insects;
- catching earwigs and slugs by laying boards in the garden at night and destroying them in the morning;
- checking plants regularly and treating for any pest at the first sign;
- removing and destroying dead or distressed foliage or flowers from the garden throughout the growing season;
- cleaning up thoroughly in the fall so pests will have fewer places to overwinter in the garden.

If insects or disease do become a serious problem, use a pesticide, following the manufacturer's recommendations. The best organic controls for most insects are insecticidal soaps, pyrethrum, and rotenone; for caterpillars, use *Bacillus thuringiensis*. The two safest broad-spectrum chemical controls are Sevin (carbaryl) and malathion. For fungus diseases, use benomyl or sulfur. There is no solution for virus diseases except to destroy the plant and control the aphid or leafhoppers that spread the disease.

Leaf miners are insects that tunnel through leaf tissue, leaving white trails which disfigure the plant but do not affect its health. They are best controlled by removing and burning the damaged foliage.

Control powdery mildew with fungicide applications or by thinning out growth to improve air circulation around plants and keeping the soil moist during summer. Avoid wetting the foliage when watering.

STARTING PERENNIALS FROM SEED

Most gardeners either buy their perennials from local or mail-order nurseries or get plants from other gardeners. Starting perennials from seed is much less usual, except for certain plants that readily grow this way. These include English daisy, delphiniums, pinks, hibiscus, foxgloves, gloriosa daisies, lupines, shasta daisy, and painted daisy.

The procedure is much the same as starting annual seeds indoors or in a greenhouse, except that there is often a two-year wait before the plants bloom. This long lag time necessitates developing a nursery area for growing the plants until they can be in the garden as well as protecting them during the winter.

Perennials have differing germination requirements, so follow the instructions on the seed packet. Use any of the specialized equipment for starting seeds, such as peat moss cubes or pellets or peat pots, plastic pots, trays, cell-paks filled with moistened soilless seed-starting mix. Sow the seeds, then handle according to the specific requirements on the packet. Some perennial seeds must have light or heat to germinate, while others need cool temperatures or darkness. Sometimes the seed coats must have special treatment, such as being nicked with a file or having boiling water poured over them. The germination time varies greatly as well. Whatever the procedure, be sure to keep the growing medium moist. Once the seeds germinate, provide bright, indirect light, either by growing under fluorescent lights, or placing in a greenhouse or lath house.

After several sets of leaves have developed, transplant the seedlings to larger pots or into a nursery bed. Shelter them with lath or continue growing in a cool greenhouse or indoors under lights for several weeks until they are actively growing again. At this time, transplant to a nursery area outdoors. Water and feed regularly during the summer. Mulch the nursery bed in late fall after the ground has frozen or cover with a cold frame.

ABOVE: *When dividing perennials, use a spading fork to dig up the entire clump, then use your hands to pull the clump into smaller pieces.*

DIVIDING PERENNIALS

As perennials spread and grow, each plant competes with itself and other plants for water, nutrients, and space. Dividing perennials, then, is a significant part of their upkeep. Division is needed either to rejuvenate an aging plant, to control the size of a plant, or to have additional plants.

Spring- and summer-blooming plants are generally divided in late summer or fall and fall-blooming plants in early spring. In areas with winters of −20°F (−28°C) or colder, division is often best accomplished in the spring, so plants have a full growing season to become established before facing the rigors of winter; the exception are the plants blooming in early spring, such as primroses, leopard's bane and lungwort.

Several days before dividing, water the bed well. For spring division, plan on keeping two to four buds or sprouts with each section; when dividing in fall or whenever in active growth, cut the plants back by half and keep at least two to four stems with each portion.

With a spading fork or spade, dig up the entire clump. If possible, use your hands to divide the clump into smaller sections. When roots are tightly ensnarled, insert two spading forks back to back in the center and press the handles toward each other, prising the clump apart. For plants with thick, carrot-like roots, use a knife to cut apart each section. If the center of the clump has not died, it is sometimes possible to use a spade to cut away portions at the outer edges of the plant.

Replenish the soil in the hole from which the clump was removed with top soil, organic matter, and a handful of 0–10–10 or similar fertilizer. Replant one or more of the divisions in the hole, if desired, and replant the others in another part of the garden, share them with friends, or throw them away. Keep the plants well watered until established again.

PROPAGATING PERENNIALS FROM STEM AND ROOT CUTTINGS

Using stem cuttings for propagation is an efficient way to get additional plants without digging up the parent plant. Generally, spring is the best time to take stem cuttings of summer-blooming plants, and early summer is best for plants blooming in spring and fall.

To take a cutting, cut a piece 4–8 in (10–20 cm) long from the top of a stalk. It is best to cut slightly below the point where leaves join the stem. Remove the lower leaves, moisten the stem end, dip in rooting hormone, and put in a pot of moistened soilless seed-starting mix. Insert a label showing the date and the name of the plant, and cover the pot with a plastic bag. Place in a warm spot with bright, indirect light. Do not let the potting mix dry out; mist the cuttings several times a day. When cuttings have rooted and new growth starts, transplant to bigger pots or to a nursery bed. When plants are large enough, transfer to the garden.

Root cuttings are mainly useful when a large number of plants are wanted. It works best with just a few perennials. In early spring, either cut off some of the outer roots without disturbing the plant or dig up the entire plant and cut up all or part of the roots.

For plants with fine roots, such as phlox, yarrow, sea holly, spurge, blanketflower, sage and Stoke's aster, cut the roots into pieces 2 in (5 cm) long and spread them horizontally over the surface of a tray of moistened potting mix. Cover them with ½ in (12 mm) more of moist mix. Keep moist until the sprouts develop, then treat the plants as seedlings.

For plants with fleshy roots, such as bee balm, bleeding heart, baby's breath, poppies and peonies, cut the roots into pieces 2–3 in (5–7.5 cm) long, keeping the top ends facing the same direction. Plant them vertically, top ends up, in moistened potting mix with ¼ in (6 mm) sticking above the soil. Keep moist until sprouts develop, then treat as seedlings.

SPECIAL USES, SITES, AND CHARACTERISTICS

PERENNIALS FOR CUT FLOWERS

Achillea YARROW
Aconitum MONKSHOOD
Adenophora LADYBELLS
Alchemilla LADY'S MANTLE
Amsonia BLUE STARS
Anchusa BUGLOSS
Anemone ANEMONE
Anthemis GOLDEN MARGUERITE
Aquilegia COLUMBINE
Asclepias BUTTERFLY WEED
Aster ASTER
Astilbe ASTILBE
Baptisia FALSE INDIGO
Bergenia BERGENIA
Campanula BELLFLOWER
Centaurea KNAPWEED
Centranthus RED VALERIAN
Chrysanthemum CHRYSANTHEMUM
Cimicifuga SNAKEROOT, BUGBANE
Clematis CLEMATIS
Coreopsis TICKSEED
Delphinium LARKSPUR
Dianthus CARNATION, PINKS
Dicentra BLEEDING HEART
Dictamnus GAS PLANT
Digitalis FOXGLOVE
Doronicum LEOPARD'S BANE
Echinacea PURPLE CONEFLOWER
Echinops GLOBE THISTLE
Erigeron FLEABANE
Eryngium SEA HOLLY
Eupatorium MIST FLOWER,
   JOE-PYE WEED
Filipendula QUEEN-OF-THE-PRAIRIE,
   QUEEN-OF-THE-MEADOW,
   DROPWORT
Gaillardia BLANKET FLOWER
Geum GEUM
Gypsophila BABY'S BREATH
Helenium SNEEZEWEED
Heliopsis FALSE SUNFLOWER
Helleborus HELLEBORE
Hesperis SWEET ROCKET
Heuchera CORAL BELLS
Hosta PLANTAIN LILY
Iris IRIS
Kniphofia TORCH LILY
Lavandula LAVENDER
Liatris GAYFEATHER
Lobelia CARDINAL FLOWER,
   GREAT BLUE LOBELIA
Lupinus LUPINE

Lychnis MALTESE CROSS,
   GERMAN CATCHFLY, ROSE CAMPION
Lysimachia GOOSENECK
   LOOSESTRIFE
Macleaya PLUME POPPY
Monarda BEE BALM
Ornamental grasses
Paeonia PEONY
Papaver ORIENTAL POPPY
Phlox PHLOX
Physostegia OBEDIENT PLANT
Platycodon BALLOON FLOWER
Primula PRIMROSE
Rudbeckia CONEFLOWER
Salvia SAGE
Scabiosa PINCUSHION FLOWER
Sedum STONECROP
Solidago GOLDENROD
Stokesia STOKES' ASTER
Thalictrum MEADOWRUE
Thermopsis CAROLINA THERMOPSIS
Veronica SPEEDWELL
Viola VIOLET

PERENNIALS FOR BOG GARDENS

Aruncus GOATSBEARD
Astilbe ASTILBE
Cimicifuga SNAKEROOT
Eupatorium JOE-PYE WEED
Ferns SENSITIVE, ROYAL AND
   CINNAMON FERNS
Filipendula QUEEN-OF-THE-PRAIRIE,
   QUEEN-OF-THE-MEADOW
Helenium SNEEZEWEED
Hibiscus ROSE MALLOW
Iris (selected varieties) IRIS
Lobelia CARDINAL FLOWER
Lysimachia LOOSESTRIFE
Lythrum PURPLE LOOSESTRIFE
Monarda BEE BALM
Physostegia OBEDIENT PLANT
Primula japonica JAPANESE
   PRIMROSE

PERENNIALS FOR ROCK GARDENS

Alchemilla LADY'S MANTLE
Aquilegia COLUMBINE
Arabis ROCKCRESS
Armeria THRIFT
Artemisia schmidtiana
   SILVER MOUND
Asarum WILD GINGER
Aubretia PURPLE ROCK CRESS
Aurinia BASKET-OF-GOLD
Bellis ENGLISH DAISY
Bergenia BERGENIA
Campanula (selected varieties)
   BELLFLOWER
Cerastium SNOW-IN-SUMMER
Dianthus PINKS
Dicentra (selected varieties)
   BLEEDING HEART
Filipendula vulgaris DROPWORT
Gaillardia 'Goblin'
   BLANKETFLOWER
Galium SWEET WOODRUFF
Geranium CRANE'S BILL
Geum GEUM
Heuchera CORAL BELLS
Hosta (selected varietes)
   PLANTAIN LILY
Iberis CANDYTUFT
Iris (selected varieties) IRIS
Lavandula LAVENDER
Linum FLAX
Phlox (selected varieties) PHLOX
Primula PRIMROSE
Sedum (selected varieties)
   STONECROP
Stachys BETONY
Veronica (selected varieties)
   SPEEDWELL
Viola VIOLA

PERENNIALS FOR FRAGRANCE

Centranthus RED VALERIAN
Cimicifuga SNAKEROOT, BUGBANE
Dianthus CARNATION, PINKS
Dictamnus GAS PLANT
Filipendula QUEEN-OF-THE-
   MEADOW, QUEEN-OF-THE-PRAIRIE
Galium SWEET WOODRUFF
Hemerocallis (selected
   varieties) DAY LILY
Hesperis DAME'S ROCKET
Hosta plantaginea FRAGRANT
   PLANTAIN LILY
Iris BEARDED IRIS
Lavandula LAVENDER
Monarda BEE BALM
Oenothera MISSOURI PRIMROSE
Paeonia PEONY
Phlox paniculata GARDEN PHLOX
Primula (selected varieties)
   PRIMROSE

PERENNIALS FOR DRIED FLOWERS

Achillea YARROW
Alchemilla LADY'S MANTLE
Anaphalis PEARLY EVERLASTING
Artemisia MUGWORT, WORMWOOD,
   SOUTHERNWOOD
Asclepias BUTTERFLY WEED
Belamcanda BLACKBERRY LILY
Cimicifuga SNAKEROOT, BUGBANE
Dictamnus GAS PLANT
Echinacea PURPLE CONEFLOWER
Echinops GLOBE THISTLE
Eryngium SEA HOLLY
Gypsophila BABY'S BREATH
Helenium SNEEZEWEED
Heliopsis FALSE SUNFLOWER
Lavandula LAVENDER
Liatris GAYFEATHER
Macleaya PLUME POPPY
Oenothera MISSOURI PRIMROSE
Ornamental grasses
Rudbeckia CONEFLOWER
Salvia SAGE
Scabiosa PINCUSHION FLOWER
Sedum STONECROP
Solidago GOLDENROD

SPECIAL USES, SITES, AND CHARACTERISTICS

PERENNIALS TO ATTRACT BUTTERFLIES AND HUMMINGBIRDS

Aquilegia COLUMBINE
Asclepias BUTTERFLY WEED
Campanula BELLFLOWER
Centaurea macrocephala GLOBE CORNFLOWER
Centranthus RED VALERIAN
Delphinium LARKSPUR
Dianthus CARNATION, PINKS
Digitalis FOXGLOVE
Echinacea PURPLE CONEFLOWER
Echinops GLOBE THISTLE
Eupatorium MIST FLOWER, JO-PYE WEED
Hemerocallis DAY LILY
Hesperis SWEET ROCKET
Heuchera CORAL BELLS
Iris BEARDED IRIS
Kniphofia TORCH LILY
Liatris GAYFEATHER
Lobelia CARDINAL FLOWER
Lupinus LUPINE
Lychnis ROSE CAMPION
Lythrum PURPLE LOOSESTRIFE
Monarda BEE BALM
Nepeta CATMINT
Papaver ORIENTAL POPPY
Phlox PHLOX
Rudbeckia CONEFLOWER
Salvia SAGE
Stachys BIG BETONY

PERENNIALS FOR MEADOW GARDENS

Achillea YARROW
Amsonia BLUE STARS
Anthemis GOLDEN MARGUERITE
Asclepias BUTTERFLY WEED
Aster ASTER
Baptisia FALSE INDIGO
Coreopsis TICKSEED
Echinacea PURPLE CONEFLOWER
Echinops GLOBE THISTLE
Erigeron FLEABANE
Eryngium SEA HOLLY
Eupatorium coelestinum MIST FLOWER
Gaillardia BLANKETFLOWER
Helenium SNEEZEWEED
Heliopsis FALSE SUNFLOWER
Hemerocallis DAY LILY
Liatris GAYFEATHER
Linum FLAX
Lobelia CARDINAL FLOWER, GREAT BLUE LOBELIA
Lychnis GERMAN CATCHFLY, ROSE CAMPION
Lysimachia LOOSESTRIFE
Lythrum PURPLE LOOSESTRIFE
Monarda BEE BALM
Oenothera MISSOURI PRIMROSE
Ornamental grasses
Physostegia OBEDIENT PLANT
Rudbeckia CONEFLOWER
Solidago GOLDENROD
Thermopsis CAROLINA THERMOPSIS

PERENNIALS FOR GROUND COVERS

Alchemilla LADY'S MANTLE
Arabis ROCKCRESS
Armeria THRIFT
Asarum WILD GINGER
Aubretia PURPLE ROCKCRESS
Aurinia BASKET-OF-GOLD
Bergenia BERGENIA
Brunnera BUGLOSS
Campanula (selected varieties) BELLFLOWER
Cerastium SNOW-IN-SUMMER
Chrysogonum GOLDEN STAR
Dianthus PINKS
Ferns
Geranium CRANESBILL
Galium SWEET WOODRUFF
Gypsophila repens CREEPING BABY'S BREATH
Heuchera CORAL BELLS
Hosta PLANTAIN LILY
Iberis CANDYTUFT
Ornamental grass BLUE FESCUE
Phlox subulata CREEPING PHLOX
Stachys LAMB'S EARS

LOW-MAINTENANCE PERENNIALS

Achillea YARROW
Aconitum MONKSHOOD
Achemilla LADY'S MANTLE
Amsonia BLUE STARS
Artemisia ARTEMISIA
Aruncus GOATSBEARD
Asclepias BUTTERFLY WEED
Astilbe ASTILBE
Aurinia BASKET-OF-GOLD
Baptisia FALSE INDIGO
Bergenia BERGENIA
Brunnera BUGLOSS
Campanula BELLFLOWER
Centaurea KNAPWEED
Chrysanthemum coccineum PAINTED DAISY
Cimicifuga SNAKEROOT
Clematis CLEMATIS
Coreopsis TICKWEED
Dicentra BLEEDING HEART
Dictamnus GAS PLANT

Doronicum LEOPARD'S BANE
Echinacea PURPLE CONEFLOWER
Echinops GLOBE THISTLE
Erigeron FLEABANE
Eryngium SEA HOLLY
Euphorbia SPURGE
Filipendula QUEEN-OF-THE-PRAIRIE, QUEEN-OF-THE-MEADOW, DROPWORT
Geranium CRANESBILL
Gypsophila BABY'S BREATH
Helenium SNEEZEWEED
Heliopsis FALSE SUNFLOWER
Helleborus HELLEBORE
Hemerocallis DAY LILY
Heuchera CORAL BELLS
Hibiscus ROSE MALLOW
Hosta PLANTAIN LILY
Iberis CANDYTUFT
Iris sibirica SIBERIAN IRIS
Liatris GAYFEATHER
Linum FLAX
Lychnis CAMPION
Lysimachia LOOSESTRIFE
Lythrum PURPLE LOOSESTRIFE
Mertensia VIRGINIA BLUEBELL
Nepeta CATMINT
Oenothera missouriensis MISSOURI PRIMROSE
Ornamental grasses
Paeonia PEONY
Papaver ORIENTAL POPPY
Physostegia OBEDIENT PLANT
Platycodon BALLOON FLOWER
Polygonatum SOLOMON'S SEAL
Pulmonaria LUNGWORT
Rudbeckia CONEFLOWER
Salvia VIOLET SAGE
Scabiosa PINCUSHION FLOWER
Sedum STONECROP
Solidago GOLDENROD
Stachys BETONY
Stokesia STOKES' ASTER
Thalictrum MEADOWRUE
Thermopsis CAROLINA THERMOPSIS
Tradescantia SPIDERWORT
Veronica SPEEDWELL

ENCYCLOPEDIA SECTION

THE PERENNIALS CHOSEN for this book are ones that have been favorites for generations as well as those that have only recently come into garden use. Besides popularity, the length of time each year the plant makes an aesthetic contribution to the garden was also considered. A plant should either bloom for a long period or be attractive for most of the the growing season. Conversely, if the foliage does become unattractive, then it should die down quickly so other plants fill in.

In this era of stress-filled lives, gardening should be a source of relaxation, not just another chore on an endless list. Maintenance, then, is of key importance. Some of the old-fashioned perennials require a lot of care but are so beloved that they are still widely grown. More and more, however, gardeners are choosing plants that have as many low-maintenance characteristics as possible. These include resistance to insects and diseases; tolerance of a wide range of soil types and moisture conditions; infrequent need for division (preferably no more than every four years); resistance to summer heat; and infrequent need for staking.

Few plants meet all of these criteria, but ones that satisfy as many as possible have been included in the following section. Another attribute was hardiness; with only a few exceptions, the plants described are hardy to at least −30°F (−34°C). Conversely, most of the plants can also be grown in areas with much warmer winter temperatures, except subtropical regions.

DEFINING BOTANICAL TERMS

Both the common and the botanical, or Latin binomial, names have been used in the plant descriptions. Just as a person's full name is necessary for proper identification, the same applies to plants. A common name for a plant in one region may be used for an entirely different plant somewhere else while Latin names are the same throughout the world.

A binomial includes the generic name, which is followed by the species name. Sometimes there is a third word, which is a subspecies or variety (var.) name.

OPPOSITE *Salvia superba* 'MAY NIGHT'

Taxonomists sometimes change botanical names, and the older forms have been included for clarification. A garden form, sport, clone, or result of a hybrid cross is called a cultivar; the cultivar name is enclosed in single quotation marks. Cultivars are usually propagated vegetatively, from divisions or cuttings, as they may or may not reproduce true from seed.

GUIDE TO USING THE ENCYCLOPEDIA SECTION

■ Perennials are arranged alphabetically by their botanical, or Latin binomial name.
■ Below each entry is a chart of symbols that provide easy reference to information on specific temperature and positioning needs, or to plants which are recommended for particular sites or uses.
■ Information relating to color, height, bloom time, soil, sun and spacing requirements for all the perennials featured in this section is tabulated for easy reference in the chart at the back of the book.

Easy care Dried flowers

Full sun Fragrant flowers

Full sun to partial shade Attract butterflies and hummingbirds

Partial shade Meadow gardens

Partial to full shade Ground cover

Heat tolerant Rock gardens

Cut flowers Bog gardens

ACHILLEA

YARROW

CERTAIN YARROWS ARE indispensable to any garden where low maintenance is a consideration. The pungently scented, feathery, gray or dark green leaves are topped with flat flower clusters for a month or more from early to midsummer, and longer if faded flowers are removed. In shades of yellow, red, pink, and white, all yarrow flowers are good for cutting and using either fresh or dried.

■ **SPECIES, VARIETIES, AND CULTIVARS** There are numerous cultivars and hybrids of varying heights of the golden, or fernleaf, yarrow (*Achillea filipendulina*). *A.* × *taygeta* grows 18 in (45 cm) tall with silvery leaves and pale yellow flowers.

Common yarrow (*A. millefolium*), also known as milfoil, is a weedy plant with off-white flowers, but selected forms with pink to red flowers are better for the garden and are good cut flowers. Plants grow 18–24 in (45–60 cm) tall with flowers 2–3 in (5–7.5 cm) across. 'Crimson Beauty', 'Fire King', and 'Red Beauty' are available cultivars.

Achillea filipendulina 'CORONATION GOLD'

A number of the new hybrid yarrows usually grow 2 ft (60 cm) tall, with broad clusters of 4-in (10-cm) flower heads. The white-flowered sneezewort (*A. ptarmica*) can be invasive and needs division every other year, but the flowers are good for cutting. Low-growing *A. tomentosa* is a rapid grower best suited to large rock gardens or as an edging.

■ **CULTIVATION AND CARE TIPS.** Yarrows grow best in full sun with average or poor, well-drained soil. If grown in rich, moist soil, they tend to become invasive. Space larger-growing types 12–18 in (30–45 cm) apart and shorter ones 10–12 in (25–30 cm) apart, either singly or in groups of three. The taller varieties may need staking. Divide every fourth year. All are hardy to −50°F (−46°C).

■ **PROPAGATION.** Division in spring, keeping four or five young shoots with each portion. Seed.

■ **PESTS AND DISEASES.** Basically trouble free, but crown gall, mildew, or rust may occur.

Achillea millefolium 'FIRE KING'

ACONITUM

MONKSHOOD

MAGNIFICENTLY ELEGANT monkshoods have much to recommend them: attractive glossy, divided foliage; wonderful spikes of unusually hooded blue flowers in late summer and early fall that are good for cutting; and a long life and infrequent need for division.

Although used medicinally, all plant parts are poisonous and care should be taken with small children.

■ **SPECIES, VARIETIES, AND CULTIVARS.** Azure monkshood (*Aconitum carmichaelii*, sometimes listed by its old name *A. fischeri*) grows about 3 ft (90 cm) tall. Hardy to −40°F (−40°C). *A. × cammarum* (also listed as *A. napellus*) has more finely divided leaves with blue to violet flowers on 3–4-ft (90-cm–1.20-m) stems in mid to late summer. Hardy to −20°F (−28°C).

■ **CULTIVATION AND CARE TIPS.** Such lushness requires a humus-rich, slightly acidic soil that is moist and well-drained. Regular watering in summer is necessary. Plants do best in cool to moderate climates but grow in hotter climates in light shade. A summer mulch in all climates is beneficial. Staking is advisable. Cut back spent flower stems to encourage growth. Plant as individual specimens 18 in (45 cm) from other plants and in the middle to back of a border.

■ **PROPAGATION.** Division in fall or early spring. Seed.

■ **PESTS AND DISEASES.** Seldom bothered, but crown rot, mildew, mosaic, or wilt may occur.

Aconitum carmichaelii

Adenophora confusa

ADENOPHORA

LADYBELLS

RESEMBLING THEIR CLOSE relatives, the campanulas, ladybells have delicate, ¾-in (18-mm), blue or purple bell-like flowers from mid to late summer on long-lived plants growing 2–3 ft (60–90 cm) tall.

■ **SPECIES, VARIETIES, AND CULTIVARS.** China-native *A. confusa* is generally shorter while the European *A. lilifolia* is slightly taller with paler, fragrant flowers.

■ **CULTIVATION AND CARE TIPS.** They grow in sun or light shade with a humus-rich, moist, well-drained soil. They do not transplant readily. Group several plants together about 12 in (30 cm) apart for greatest effect. Hardy to −40°F (−40°C).

■ **PROPAGATION.** Seed. Cuttings.

■ **PESTS AND DISEASES.** Seldom bothered.

Alchemilla mollis

ALCHEMILLA
LADY'S MANTLE

THE SPREADING MOUNDS of velvety, rounded gray-green leaves with fan-like pleats and serrated edges have made lady's mantle a staple for the front of a border. The frothy masses of chartreuse flowers lasting several weeks in early summer are delightful in fresh or dried bouquets. Sold variously as *Alchemilla mollis* or *A. vulgaris*, plants grow 12 in (30 cm) tall with the flower stems extending 6 in (15 cm) above.

■ **CULTIVATION AND CARE TIPS.** They prefer partial shade, but full sun is tolerated in climates with cool summers. In mild-winter areas, the plants are evergreen. Moist, well-drained, humus-rich soil is needed. Plants readily reseed, so remove faded flowers if new plants are not wanted. Plants seldom need to be divided, but can be after the fourth year if desired. Plant in groups of three, spaced 12 in (30 cm) apart or use mass plantings as a ground cover. Hardy to −40°F (−40°C).

■ **PROPAGATION.** Division in spring or fall. Seed.

■ **PESTS AND DISEASES.** Seldom bothered.

BLUE STARS

THIS LOW MAINTENANCE perennial has loose, rounded clusters of pale blue, ½-in (12-mm), star-shaped flowers on stiff 2–3-ft (60–90-cm) stems that provide a gentle contrast to other stronger-colored flowers in spring and early summer. They are good for cutting if the stems are seared in a flame to prevent "bleeding." The narrow, glossy, willow-like leaves remain attractive all season long before turning yellow in the fall. The most readily available species is *A. tabernaemontana*.

■ **CULTIVATION AND CARE TIPS.** They grow in average moist or dry soil in full sun or light shade. Adding humus to the soil and mulching will encourage best growth, but don't overfertilize or growth will be too open. Plants form clumps 18–24 in (45–60 cm) wide and should be planted singly or in small groups 18 in (45 cm) apart toward the middle of a border. Hardy to −40°F (−40°C).

■ **PROPAGATION.** Division in spring. Seed.

■ **PESTS AND DISEASES.** Seldom bothered.

Amsonia tabernaemontana

Anaphalis cinnamomea

ANAPHALIS

PEARLY EVERLASTING

THROUGHOUT SUMMER small clusters of pearly white flowers on 2-ft (60-cm) stems provide material for dried flower arrangements. Cut when the flowers just begin to show their centers, first putting in a vase of water for several hours, then hanging upside down in a dark, dry place. It is one of the few silver- or gray-foliaged plants able to grow in moist soil.

■ **SPECIES, VARIETIES, AND CULTIVARS.** *Anaphalis triplinervis* forms 12–18-in (30–45-cm) mounds of spear-shaped gray leaves that become greener when the plant blooms. *A. cinnamomea* (also listed as *A. yedoen-*

sis) has narrower leaves and woolly stems. It is a better choice for dry soils.

■ **CULTIVATION AND CARE TIPS.** They grow best in moist but well-drained soil in full sun to light shade. Plant as single specimens or in groups of three, spacing 12 in (30 cm) apart. Hardy to −40°F (−40°C).

■ **PROPAGATION.** Division in spring, usually every four years.

■ **PESTS AND DISEASES.** Seldom bothered.

Anchusa azurea

ANCHUSA

BUGLOSS, ALKANET

RESEMBLING FORGET-ME-NOTS, bugloss is favored for the airy sprays of intensely colored, dark blue flowers in bloom over a long period in summer. There are a number of varieties of *Anchusa azurea*.

■ **CULTIVATION AND CARE TIPS.** They prefer deep, humus-rich, well-drained soil with full sun or very light shade. Cutting back after flowering encourages a second blooming. The coarse, hairy foliage may flop unless staked. Plants do not live very long but self-sow readily; Division is needed every two to three years. Plant singly or in groups of three near the back of a border, spacing plants 18 in (45 cm) apart. Hardy to −40°F (−40°C).

■ **PROPAGATION.** Division or root cuttings in spring or fall. Seed.

■ **PESTS AND DISEASES.** Leafhoppers; mosaic; rust.

124

ANEMONE

JAPANESE ANEMONE, GRAPE-LEAVED ANEMONE

ANEMONES ARE A diverse group of plants, including both perennials and bulbs, with some best suited for woodland or rock gardens.

■ **SPECIES, VARIETIES, AND CULTIVARS.** The fall-blooming varieties of Japanese anemone (*A.* × *hybrida*, also called *A. hupehensis* var. *japonica*) and grape-leaved anemone (*A. vitifolia* or *A. tomentosa* 'Robustissima') are some of the most handsome perennials for the garden. The flowers are in shades of pink or white on slender, swaying, 2–3-ft (60–90-cm) branched stems above 2-ft (60-cm) mounds of deeply lobed, dark green leaves. The grape-leaved anemone blooms a month earlier, and is an excellent plant naturalized among shrubs. Of the spring-flowering anemones, the pasque flower (*A. pulsatilla*, also known as *Pulsatilla vulgaris*) has unusual, fern-like leaves covered with silken white hairs and fuzzy seed heads. Plants grow 8–12 in (20–30 cm) tall. Hardy to −30°F (−34°C). The snowdrop anemone (*A. sylvestris*) blooms a little later in spring with fragrant white flowers on 12-in (30-cm) plants.

The rapidly spreading roots quickly form a colony.

■ **CULTIVATION AND CARE TIPS.** Fall-blooming anemones must have partial shade or full sun in a location out of wind and a humus-rich soil that is moist in summer but well-drained. The grape-leaved anemone is slightly more tolerant of heat, cold, sun, and dry soil. Hardy to −20°F (−28°C), plants develop slowly even with ideal conditions, but they are long-lived and should not be moved. A loose winter mulch of straw, oak leaves or evergreen boughs is recommended for Japanese anemones. They are best when planted in groups of three, spaced 18 in (45 cm) apart. Spring-blooming anemones need full sun to partial shade with well-drained soil and self-sow readily, spaced 8 in (20 cm) apart. Hardy to −30°F (−34°C). Snowdrop anemones grow in partial shade with humus-rich, well-drained soil. Hardy to −40°F (−40°C)

■ **PROPAGATION.** Root cuttings or division in fall.

■ **PESTS AND DISEASES.** Blister beetle; leaf spot; collar rot.

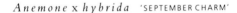

Anemone x *hybrida* 'SEPTEMBER CHARM'

Anthemis tinctoria 'KELWAYII'

ANTHEMIS

GOLDEN MARGUERITE

SUNNY YELLOW DAISY-LIKE flowers excellent for cutting, ferny aromatic foliage, a tolerance of hot, dry conditions and sandy, slightly alkaline soil are the advantages of marguerites (*Anthemis tinctoria*).

■ **SPECIES, VARIETIES, AND CULTIVARS.** *A. marschalliana* (also called *A. biebersteiniana*) forms dense 10-in (25-cm) tall mats of feathery, silver foliage perfect for the rock garden. Plant 12 in (30 cm) apart. Hardy to −30°F (−34°C). St John's chamomile (*A. sanctijohannis*) is similar to golden marguerite but has bright orange flowers and gray-green leaves. Also an excellent cut flower. Hardy to −20°F (−28°C).

■ **CULTIVATION AND CARE TIPS.** Plants tend to develop dead areas in the center and must be divided every other year or so. Staking may be necessary with the 2-ft (60-cm) plants. Grow in full sun in average, well-drained soil, spacing plants 15 in (38 cm) apart. Deadhead regularly to prolong blooming.

■ **PROPAGATION.** Division in spring. Seed.

■ **PESTS AND DISEASES.** Seldom bothered except by mildew when air circulation is poor.

COLUMBINE

THESE OLD FAVORITES deserve garden space for their unusually shaped early summer flowers. The cup and spur may be the same color or in contrasting colors. Good for cutting, the flowers may also be double.

■ **SPECIES, VARIETIES, AND CULTIVARS.** 'Mc-Kanna's Giants' has become one of the most popular strains since its introduction in 1955. There is an extensive color range of large flowers with sturdy growth 30–36 in (75–90 cm) tall. Especially notable is the Japanese fan columbine (*Aquilegia flabellata*) with its bright blue flowers with spurs curving prominently inward and the fan-shaped, gray-blue leaves on the 15-in (38-cm) plants. Its dwarf and white-flowered forms grow 8–12 in (20–30 cm) tall.

■ **CULTIVATION AND CARE TIPS.** These graceful plants are useful in sunny perennial plantings in cooler summer climates, but in most areas they do best in lightly shaded borders and woodlands. The shorter types are excellent for rock gardens. Well-drained soil is a must, but an overly dry soil is not tolerated. Plants readily self-sow. When planting, space 12 in (30 cm) apart. Hardy to −40°F (−40°C).

■ **PROPAGATION.** Seed.

■ **PESTS AND DISEASES.** Leaf miners.

Aquilegia flabellata 'NANA'

Arabis caucasica

ROCK CRESS

Although rock cresses are usually grown in the rock garden, two species are also of particular merit as an edging or accent plant along walls, banks, or other landscape features.

■ **SPECIES, VARIETIES, AND CULTIVARS.** Creeping 8-in (20-cm) mounds of soft gray-green leaves mark *Arabis caucasica*, while *A. procurrens* forms a compact mat of tiny, glossy evergreen leaves. Both bear loose spikes of ½-in (12-mm), fragrant white flowers in spring.

■ **CULTIVATION AND CARE TIPS.** They must have loose, well-drained, limy soil of only average fertility and full sun. Cut back the flowers after blooming. Set plants 8–12 in (20–30 cm) apart. Hardy to −40°F (−40°C).

■ **PROPAGATION.** Division in spring. Seed.

■ **PESTS AND DISEASES.** Aphids; club root; leaf spot; mildew. Will rot in areas with hot, humid summers.

ARMERIA

THRIFT, SEA PINK

NEAT, GRASSLIKE CLUMPS of evergreen leaves bear leafless stalks with pink or white 1-in (2.5-cm), globe-shaped flower heads in spring and early summer. Thrifts are excellent for the rock garden, between flagstones, along walls, or at the front of a border.

■ **SPECIES, VARIETIES, AND CULTIVARS.** A few of the varieties of the 6-in (15-cm) *Armeria maritima* are worth considering, such as the white 'Alba', cherry red 'Dusseldorf Pride', the intense red 'Bloodstone', and the deep pink 'Vindictive'. Plantain thrift (*A. pseudo-ameria*, or *A. plantaginea*) forms more strapping clumps to 18 in (45 cm) tall but still with narrow leaves.

■ **CULTIVATION AND CARE TIPS.** They must have average to sandy, well-drained soil in full sun. Set plants 8–12 in (20–30 cm) apart. Divide every three years. Deadhead regularly. Hardy to −40°F (−40°C).

■ **PROPAGATION.** Division in spring. Seed. Basal cuttings in late summer.

■ **PESTS AND DISEASES.** Seldom bothered.

Armeria maritima

Aruncus dioicus

ARTEMISIA

MUGWORT, WORMWOOD, SOUTHERNWOOD

THESE SILVER- OR gray-leaved plants are mostly grown for the effect of the foliage. Only sweet mugwort, *Artemisia lactiflora*, is grown for its masses of tiny, creamy white, fragrant blooms, borne on 4–6-ft (1.20–1.80-m) tall plants in midsummer.

■ **SPECIES, VARIETIES, AND CULTIVARS.** Avoid common mugwort (*A. vulgaris*) and Roman wormwood (*A. pontica*) because both are highly invasive. Among the most widely sought of silver-foliaged plants is *A. schmidtiana* 'Silver Mound'. The feathery 12-in (30-cm) mounds spread up to 18 in (45 cm) across. Trimming plants back before they flower lessens the tendency to open in the middle. Plants may also rot in hot, humid climates. Southernwood (*A. abrotanum*) and wormwood (*A. absinthium*) grow 18–24 in (45–60 cm) tall with finely divided gray leaves. Both dry readily for flower arrangements and wreaths as well as use in moth repellent bags. Beach wormwood (*A. stellerana*) is a tough, adaptable plant; it grows 12–18 in (30–45 cm) tall.

■ **CULTIVATION AND CARE TIPS.** They grow easily in full sun in dry, well-drained soils. Set plants 1–2 ft (30–60 cm) apart. Hardy to −30°F (−34°C).

■ **PROPAGATION.** Division in spring. Cuttings.

■ **PESTS AND DISEASES.** Seldom bothered.

Artemisia absinthium 'LAMBROOK SILVER'

ARUNCUS

GOATSBEARD

DESERVING TO BE more widely grown, goatsbeard (*Aruncus dioicus*, also known as *A. sylvester*) is a handsome, large, shrubby plant for the back of a border, the center of a bed, among shrubs, in a wildflower garden, or beside a pool. Plants grow 3 ft (90 cm) or more across and 5 ft (1.50 m) or taller with magnificent creamy white, feathery clusters of tiny flowers in early summer. The leaves are segmented and stems branch readily. The variety 'Kneiffii' has small, narrow leaves, giving it a delicately textured appearance, and only grows 2–3 ft (60–90 cm) tall.

■ **CULTIVATION AND CARE TIPS.** Long-lived, they grow best in partial shade and tolerate a wide range of soil conditions, but prefer a humus-rich, moist soil. Plants will tolerate full sun if soil is kept consistently moist. Plants seldom need staking, neither are they invasive. Set plants 24–30 in (60–75 cm) apart. Cut the stems off to several inches (cm) tall in the fall. Hardy to −30°F (−34°C).

■ **PROPAGATION.** Although sometimes difficult and seldom needed, division in spring or fall, if desired. Seed.

■ **PESTS AND DISEASES.** Seldom bothered, except occasionally by sawflies or caterpillars in spring.

129

Asarum europaeum

ASARUM
WILD GINGER

FORMING A DENSE MAT of shiny, heart-shaped leaves 6 in (15 cm) tall, European wild ginger (*A. europaeum*) is an excellent ground cover for fully to partially shaded areas. In areas with milder winters, the glossy foliage remains evergreen. Wild ginger derives the name from the aromatic scent of the foliage and roots when crushed. It is seldom invasive. In spring, purple-brown, bell-shaped flowers 1 in (2.5 cm) or less across bloom at ground level. A wild ginger native to North America (*A. canadense*) has dull green, deciduous leaves.

■ **CULTIVATION AND CARE TIPS.** Besides shade, they must have moist, well-drained, humus-rich soil to grow well. Set plants 8–12 in (20–30 cm) apart and 1 in (2.5 cm) deep. Hardy to −20°F (−28°C).

■ **PROPAGATION.** Division in spring.

■ **PESTS AND DISEASES.** Seldom bothered except where slugs and snails are a problem.

ASCLEPIAS
BUTTERFLY WEED

THE BRIGHT ORANGE, red, or yellow clusters of flowers in midsummer are true to their name, butterfly weed (*A. tuberosa*). These long-lived, easy-care plants are related to the milkweeds, and in the fall they form similar canoe-shaped pods that are useful in dried arrangements. Butterfly weed can be used as a cut flower, but the stems must be seared in a candle flame to stop the milky sap from flowing. Stocky-stemmed with long, narrow, bristly leaves, the plants grow 2–3 ft (60–90 cm) tall with the clusters of stems branching toward the top. They are very variable as to flower shade and blooming time.

■ **CULTIVATION AND CARE TIPS.** Drought-tolerant due to its taproot, it grows best in almost any sandy to average well-drained soil in full sun. Plants are slow to emerge in the spring, so mark their location well. Plant 12 in (30 cm) apart in the spring or fall when the plant is dormant, setting the taproot vertically with the point where the stems emerge 1–2 in (2.5–5 cm) below the soil surface. Hardy to −40°F (−40°C).

■ **PROPAGATION.** Seed. Division or root cuttings in early spring.

■ **PESTS AND DISEASES.** Seldom bothered.

Asclepias tuberosa

Aster x *frikartii*

ASTER

ASTER, MICHAELMAS DAISY

Asters are an indispensable part of the summer and fall garden, with the most popular garden forms growing 1–6 ft (30 cm–1.80 m) tall. All have daisy-like flowers, usually with yellow centers and blue, lavender, purple, pink, red, or white petals.

■ **SPECIES, VARIETIES, AND CULTIVARS.** *Aster × frikartii* is considered one of the best perennials. The open bushes grow 2–3 ft (60–90 cm) tall with fragrant, 2–3-in (5–7.5-cm) lavender blue flowers produced over a long period in summer and fall; these are excellent cut flowers. Although hardy to −20°F (−28°C), mulching with evergreen boughs is necessary in areas with −10°F (−23°C) or colder temperatures and soil must be well-drained. Tolerant of wet soils, the New England aster (*A. novae-angliae*) has hairy, gray-green leaves and forms large clumps with stiff, woody stems growing 3–6 ft (90 cm–1.80 m) tall. Long-blooming during the fall, the deep purple flowers are 1–2 in (2.5–5 cm) across and close at night. The New York aster (*A. novi-belgi*), and its many hybrids usually grow 1–4 ft (30 cm–1.20 m) tall. Plants bloom during fall and make excellent cut flowers. In areas with a long growing season, pinch out the growing tips twice by midsummer to make plants bushy. Stake taller varieties.

■ **CULTIVATION AND CARE TIPS.** They do best in full sun in moist but well-drained soil that is average to humus-rich. Mulch in late spring to retain soil moisture and water during droughts. Deadhead regularly as plants readily self-sow but do not stay true to type and can become weedy. Cut stems when flowering is over in fall. Stake tall-growing varieties. Set plants 12–18 in (30–45 cm) apart. Asters do not grow well in hot, semi-tropical coastal climates. Most varieties hardy to −30°F (−34°C).

■ **PROPAGATION.** Division every other year is necessary in spring or fall with most hybrids. Cuttings. Seed.

■ **PESTS AND DISEASES.** Powdery mildew; Japanese beetles; slugs; caterpillars.

Astilbe x *arendsii* 'PEACH BLOSSOM'

ASTILBE

ASTILBE

ASTILBES ARE ONE OF the most favored, easily grown and long-lived perennials for shaded areas. Most plants have neat clumps of segmented, dark green leaves. Depending on the cultivar, flowering is from early to late summer. The feathery spires of tiny flowers in shades of pink, red, rose, and white may be used for cutting.

■ **SPECIES, VARIETIES, AND CULTIVARS.** A group of hybrids, *Astilbe × arendsii* is the most widely available. Most of the cultivars grow 2–3 ft (60–90 cm) tall with dark green or reddish foliage. The creeping *A. chinensis* 'Pumila' forms a dense mat with magenta-pink flowers growing 12 in (30 cm) tall. *A. taquetii* 'Superba' grows 3–4 ft (90 cm–1.20 m) tall with broad, bronze-green leaves and tall, narrow spires of magenta-pink flowers; it is the last astilbe to bloom and is the most heat- and drought-tolerant type.

■ **CULTIVATION AND CARE TIPS.** They prefer partial shade with moist but well-drained, humus-rich soil and extra fertilization. In cooler climates, full sun is acceptable. Plant 12–18 in (30–45 cm) apart. Cut back in late fall or early spring. Hardy to −30°F (−34°C).

■ **PROPAGATION.** Division in early spring every three years yields largest growth and best flowers.

■ **PESTS AND DISEASES.** Seldom bothered, although Japanese beetles, slugs, and snails can be a problem.

PURPLE ROCK CRESS

A SPLENDID STAPLE of the spring garden, purple rock cress (*Aubretia deltoidea*) is in its glory used at the front of a border, tumbling out of a stone wall, in a rock garden, or among flagstones. Forming 6-in (15-cm) tall mats of downy, gray-green leaves that spread to 12 in (30 cm) or more across, the ½-in (12-mm) or larger flowers may be purple, rose, red, or lavender, depending on the cultivar.

■ **CULTIVATION AND CARE TIPS.** It thrives in full sun but tolerates partial shade and needs sandy, well-drained soil containing lime and a cool, moist climate for best growth. In areas with hot summers, plants are short-lived. Shear the plants back after flowering, except ones in walls, which should just be deadheaded. Space 6–8 in (15–20 cm) apart. Hardy to −20°F (−28°C).

■ **PROPAGATION.** Division in fall. Cuttings in fall and overwintered in a greenhouse or coldframe. Seed.

■ **PESTS AND DISEASES.** Seldom bothered.

Aubretia deltoidea

AURINIA

BASKET-OF-GOLD

THE GOLDEN SUNSHINE of spring seems to have come to earth in basket-of-gold, *A. saxatilis* (also known as *Alyssum saxatile*). Easily grown, the dense, 12-in (30-cm) mounds of hairy gray-green leaves are covered with tiny, bright yellow flowers in early spring. Used as an edging to paths or steps, at the front of a border, in a rock garden, or spilling over stone walls, it is a perfect accompaniment to spring bulbs. Besides the species, there are varieties with variegated leaves, double flowers, dwarf growth, and flowers in various shades of yellow.

■ **CULTIVATION AND CARE TIPS.** For best growth, they need full sun and poor to average to sandy, very well-drained soil. Do not fertilize as rich soil causes plants to be open and sprawling. Plants may be short-lived in areas with hot, humid summers. Shear plants by one-third to one-half after flowering to encourage compact new growth. Space plants 8–12 in (20–30 cm) apart. Hardy to −30°F (−34°C).

■ **PROPAGATION.** Division in spring. Cuttings in summer. Seed.

■ **PESTS AND DISEASES.** Club root kills feeder roots and plants must be dug up and destroyed. Leaf rot in humid climates. Flea beetles.

Aurinia saxatilis

Baptisia australis

BELAMCANDA
BLACKBERRY LILY

T HE IRIS-LIKE PLANTS of blackberry lily (*B. chinensis*) grow 30 in (75 cm) tall. In midsummer thin, branching stalks bear clusters of 2-in (5-cm), yellow-orange flowers marked with red-purple dots. Fading flowers form seed pods that open to reveal shiny black seeds resembling blackberries; these are good for dried arrangements. Plants readily self-sow, but seedlings are easily pulled if not wanted. *B. flabellata*, grows 12 in (30 cm) tall and has yellow, unspeckled flowers.

■ **CULTIVATION AND CARE TIPS.** Readily growing in full sun to partial shade and tolerating average to humus-rich, well-drained soils, set plants 1 in (2.5 cm) deep and 12 in (30 cm) apart. Use as a specimen in the middle of a border. Plants are long-lived and dividing is seldom necessary. Hardy to −20°F (−28°C).

■ **PROPAGATION.** Seed. Division of rhizomes in spring or fall.

■ **PESTS AND DISEASES.** Seldom bothered, except very occasionally by iris borers.

Belamcanda chinensis

BAPTISIA
FALSE INDIGO

A LUSH, ELEGANT, shrubby plant, false indigo (*B. australis*) has sturdy, upright, 3–4-ft (90 cm–1.20 m) branching stems with blue-green leaves and pea-like, 1-in (2.5-cm), deep blue flowers. After blooming in early summer, the seedpods are also attractive, and both flowers and seedpods are good for cutting.

■ **CULTIVATION AND CARE TIPS.** Long-lived and never invasive, it is somewhat difficult to transplant so choose its location well. Tolerant of dry soil because of its taproot, it grows in full sun to partial shade in average to humus-rich, well-drained soil. Space plants 2 ft (60 cm) apart. Hardy to −40°F (−40°C).

■ **PROPAGATION.** Sow seed outdoors as soon as ripened or in the spring.

■ **PESTS AND DISEASES.** Seldom bothered.

Bellis perennis

BELLIS

ENGLISH DAISY

THE ENGLISH DAISY (*B. perennis*) is often grown as a biennial. It is a perennial nonetheless and beloved as a spring- and early-summer accent for the border or rock garden. There are many varieties, with the 1–2-in (2.5–5-cm) flowers in shades of red, rose, pink and white, and either as singles or doubles. Most types grow 3–6 in (7.5–15 cm) tall with the flower stalks emerging from the crown of dark green leaves.

■ **CULTIVATION AND CARE TIPS.** It grows well in sun and tolerates partial shade. A humus-rich, moist but well-drained soil is best. Space plants 6 in (15 cm) apart. Hardy to −40°F (−40°C), but plants need a winter mulch in areas with −20°F (−28°C) and colder.

■ **PROPAGATION.** Division every year in early fall. Seeds sown outdoors in late spring for bloom the following year or started indoors in midwinter.

■ **PESTS AND DISEASES.** Seldom bothered.

BERGENIA

BERGENIA

GROWN BOTH FOR ITS foliage and its spring-blooming flowers, bergenia can be used at the front of flower beds and borders, massed along paths, or used as a ground cover under shrubs and trees. The cabbage-like leaves are often evergreen, sometimes turning bronze in winter, and are used in flower arrangements. The clusters of small pink, magenta or white flowers are borne on thick, leafless stalks, which should be removed when flowers fade. Plants grow 12 in (30 cm) tall and as wide, spreading slowly by creeping rhizomes.

■ **SPECIES, VARIETIES, AND CULTIVARS.** The two most widely grown species are the heart-leaved bergenia (*B. cordifolia*) and the slightly smaller, winter-blooming bergenia (*B. crassifolia*). There are a number of excellent hybrid cultivars available.

■ **CULTIVATION AND CARE TIPS.** They grow well in light shade in hotter climates or in full sun in cooler areas and if soil is kept moist; otherwise they tolerate a wide range of soil types. Richer soil will require plants to be divided every three to four years. Space plants 12 in (30 cm) apart. A winter mulch may be beneficial in areas with lows of −20°F (−28°C) and colder.

■ **PROPAGATION.** Division in spring or fall, with each start having a 3–4-in (7.5–10-cm) piece of rhizome. Seed.

■ **PESTS AND DISEASES.** Slugs and snails.

Bergenia 'ABENDGLUT' ('EVENING GLOW')

SIBERIAN BUGLOSS

ROUGH, HEART-SHAPED leaves and blue forget-me-not-like flowers in spring make this a useful, low-maintenance, long-lived specimen plant in a border or rock garden or as a ground cover under trees and shrubs. The neat clumps grow 12–18 in (30–45 cm) tall. Named varieties of *B. macrophylla* (also listed as *Anchusa myosotidiflora*) are available, including variegated-leaf forms. These must be propagated by division; they will not come true to seed. Remove any solid green leaves from variegated types or they will take over.

■ **CULTIVATION AND CARE TIPS.** Although tolerant of full sun and a wide range of soils, it does best in humus-rich, moist but well-drained soil in partial shade. Remove faded flowering stems, or leave if self-seeding is desired. Space plants 12 in (30 cm) apart. Hardy to −40°F (−40°C).

■ **PROPAGATION.** Seldom necessary, but division is possible in spring or fall. Seed.

■ **PESTS AND DISEASES.** Slugs.

Brunnera macrophylla

BELLFLOWER

AN INVALUABLE GROUP of perennials, the bellflowers offer an amazing assortment of plant sizes and shapes for use in beds, borders, walls and rock gardens. The predominant flower color is blue, although white, pink, and purple forms exist. The taller types make excellent cut flowers. Most types look best when planted in groups of three. Deadhead regularly. A loose mulch of oak leaves or evergreen boughs will help to protect plant crowns from winter injury.

■ **SPECIES, VARIETIES, AND CULTIVARS.** Carpathian harebell (*Campanula carpatica*) grows 8–12 in (20–30 cm) tall, forming broad, trailing clumps of small heart-shaped leaves. The 1–2-in (2.5–5-cm) violet-blue or white cup-shaped flowers bloom throughout summer on wiry stems. Plant 10 in (25 cm) apart. Start from seed or divide in spring. Hardy to −40°F (−40°C). Clustered bellfower (*C. glomerata*) grows 1–3 ft (30–90 cm) tall with clusters of 1-in (2.5-cm) purple or white flowers at the ends of erect stems from early to mid-summer. Foliage is coarse and hairy. Space plants 2 ft (60 cm) apart, and divide every other year. Tolerant of wet soil. Plants may become invasive when grown in shade. Hardy to −40°F (−40°C). Milky bellflower (*C. lactiflora*) grows 3–5 ft (90 cm–1.50 m) tall with pale blue, violet blue, pink, or white 1-in (2.5-cm), bell-shaped flowers borne on long stiff spikes in summer. Staking may be necessary. One of the easiest bellflowers to grow, space plants 12–18 in (30–45 cm) apart. Hardy to −20°F (−28°C).

Great bellflower (*C. latifolia*) forms bold clumps of rough leaves and grows 3–4 ft (90 cm–1.20 m) tall but does not usually need staking. It is more tolerant of light shade and moist soil than most bellflowers. The 2-in (5-cm) summer-blooming flowers are purple-blue or white. Plants readily self-sow. Hardy to −30°F (−34°C). The biennial Canterbury bells (*C. medium*) and its popular cup-and-saucer form, *C. m.* var. *calycanthema*, are the showiest bellflowers. The summer-blooming 2–3-in (5–7.5-cm) flowers may be single or double, and white, purple, blue, or pink on stems 15–30 in (38–75 cm) tall. Set plants 12 in (30 cm) apart. Hardy to −30°F (−34°C). Peach-leaved bellflower (*C. persici-*

Campanula lactiflora

folia) forms clumps of narrow leaves with 2–3 ft (60–90 cm) tall flower spikes. There are numerous cultivars with 1–2-in (2.5–5-cm) flowers in shades of blue or white and either single or double bells. Divide plants in spring every two or three years, setting plants 18 in (45 cm) apart. If desired, allow to naturalize in the garden. Hardy to −30°F (−34°C). Serbian bellflower (*C. poscharskyana*) is a vigorous, drought-tolerant, spreading plant forming large 6–12-in (15–30-cm) tall mats with abundant 1-in (2.5-cm), bell-shaped lavender-blue flowers throughout summer. It may become invasive. Divide in spring or grow from seed, setting plants 12 in (30 cm) apart. Hardy to −40°F (−40°C). Bluebells, bluebells-of-Scotland, or harebell (*C. rotundifolia*) form dainty tufts 6–12 in (15–30 cm) tall. The slender flower stems bear lavender-blue or white 1-in (2.5-cm), bell-shaped flowers throughout summer. Plants can readily self-sow. Divide in spring or start from seed, setting plants 8–12 in (20–30 cm) apart. Hardy to −40°F (−40°C).

■ **CULTIVATION AND CARE TIPS.** Generally, they are easily grown and quite adaptable. Unless otherwise noted, they thrive not only in full sun but also in light shade, especially in hot climates. The preferable soil is humus-rich and moist but well-drained. Most types look best when planted in groups of three. Deadhead regularly for recurrent blooming. A loose mulch of oak leaves or evergreen boughs will help to protect plant crowns from winter injury.

■ **PROPAGATION.** Plant seed of biennial types every year. Species can be started from seed. Most named varieties must be propagated from cuttings or division in spring, as they do not usually come true from seed. Most bellflowers need dividing only every third or fourth year, if at all.

■ **PESTS AND DISEASES.** Slugs; snails; aphids; thrips. Rust disease on Carpathian, milky, and peach-leaved bellflowers. Leaf spot on Canterbury bells and peach-leaved bellflower. Crown rot if water is allowed to stand around roots.

Campanula medium

Centaurea macrocephala

KNAPWEED, PERENNIAL CORNFLOWER

THREE SPECIES OF KNAPWEED are particularly eye-catching additions to the perennial garden and tolerant of neglect as well. Each has strongly colored, thistle-like or fringed flowers that are excellent for cutting.

■ **SPECIES, VARIETIES, AND CULTIVARS.** Persian cornflower (*C. hypoleuca*, also listed as *C. dealbata*) blooms over a long period at the height of summer with 2-in (5-cm) vivid red-violet flowers centered with white. Spreading rapidly, plants grow 2 ft (60 cm) tall with coarsely cut leaves, dark green above and downy white beneath. Hardy to −40°F (−40°C). Attracting butterflies, globe cornflower (*C. macrocephala*) blooms for a short period in midsummer, bearing 3-in (7.5-cm) bright yellow flowers that are useful cut, fresh or dried. The bold 4-ft (1.20-m) plants have large, coarse leaves and make a good specimen plant. Hardy to −40°F

(−40°C). Mountain bluets or Montana cornflowers (*C. montana*) have 3-in (7.5-cm), deep violet-blue flowers in late spring and early summer. White and dark pink varieties are available. Plants grow 2 ft (60 cm) tall with downy, silver-gray leaves, and spread rapidly by self-sowing and underground stems. This is an excellent plant for a meadow garden or as a filler among early flowers. Hardy to −30°F (−34°C).

■ **CULTIVATION AND CARE TIPS.** They grow easily in full sun and average, well-drained soil, with plants set 18 in (45 cm) apart.

■ **PROPAGATION.** Division in spring every three years.

■ **PESTS AND DISEASES.** Sometimes bothered by rust in late summer; cut plants back to the ground.

CENTRANTHUS

RED VALERIAN, JUPITER'S BEARD, KEYS OF HEAVEN

*R*ED VALERIAN *(C. ruber*, sometimes listed as *Kentranthus ruber* or *Valeriana ruber*) grows readily, especially in cool-summer areas, and blooms for much of the summer. The large, showy heads of small red, pink, or white fragrant flowers bloom again if the spent stems are cut back. They are excellent as cut flowers and attract butterflies. The bushy plants grow to 3 ft (90 cm) tall with blue- or gray-green leaves. Although not long-lived, red valerian is easily propagated and plants self-sow readily, except for the white-flowered type. It is effective grown toward the middle of a perennial border, along stone walls and in rock gardens.

■ **CULTIVATION AND CARE TIPS.** It grows in average, well-drained soil in full sun to partial shade. In poor soil, plants will be shorter; in poorly drained soil they will probably not survive the winter. Set plants 12–18 in (30–45 cm) apart. Hardy to −20°F (−28°C).

■ **PROPAGATION.** Division in spring every three or four years. Basal cuttings in early summer. Self-sow.

■ **PESTS AND DISEASES.** Seldom bothered.

Centranthus ruber

Cerastium tomentosum

CERASTIUM

SNOW-IN-SUMMER

*D*ENSE MATS OF DOWNY, silvery gray, fine-textured foliage and star-shaped pure white flowers make snow-in-summer (*C. tomentosum*) a popular choice for planting in stone walls, in rock gardens, as an edging, or as a ground cover. Plants grow 6 in (15 cm) tall and spread 2 ft (60 cm), and can become invasive. The masses of ¾-in (18-mm) flowers cover the plants in early summer.

■ **SPECIES, VARIETIES, AND CULTIVARS.** Several varieties are available, including 'Silver Carpet' and 'Yo Yo'.

■ **CULTIVATION AND CARE TIPS.** It grows rampantly in full sun and poor to average garden soil; good drainage is essential. Shear plants lightly after flowering to prevent self-sowing. Set plants 12 in (30 cm) apart. Hardy to −40°F (−40°C).

■ **PROPAGATION.** Division in spring or fall. Softwood cuttings taken in summer after flowering. Seed.

■ **PESTS.** Seldom bothered, but foliage may become unattractive by fall.

Chrysanthemum x *morifolium*

CHRYSANTHEMUM

CHRYSANTHEMUM, DAISY

SYNONYMOUS WITH FALL, the garden, or florists' chrysanthemum (C. × *morifolium*) is a glorious addition to the garden in its innumerable shapes, colors, and sizes. Plants grow 1–4 ft (30 cm–1.20 m) tall and can be rounded or tall and narrow in shape, usually with small gray-green leaves. The 1–6-in (2.5–15-cm) daisy-like flowers may be single, double or pompons, with some having special shapes described as button, spoon, quill or spider. All colors except blue have been developed. Depending on the size, chrysanthemums can be used singly, in groups, or massed in borders, beds and rock gardens, or used as an edging.

■ **SPECIES, VARIETIES, AND CULTIVARS.** Pyrethrum, or painted daisy (*C. coccineum*) has 3-in (7.5-cm), single or double daisy-like pink, red, or white flowers with yellow centers on tall, single stems from early to midsummer. They are excellent as cut flowers. Growing 1–3 ft (30–90 cm) tall, the plants have ferny, dark green leaves and are best planted in groups of three.

Shasta daisy (*C. maximum*) has 3–5-in (7.5–12.5-cm) single or double flowers during the summer that are excellent for cutting. The long, narrow, shiny leaves and stems form 1–3 ft (30–90 cm) clumps. The long-blooming, daisy-like flowers of feverfew (*C. parthenium*, also called *Tanacetum parthenium* and *Matricaria parthenium)* are 1 in (2.5 cm) or less across and white or yellow, single or double, and superb for cutting. The plants can grow to 3 ft (90 cm) tall and sprawl unless sheared back when 12 in (30 cm) tall. Feverfew will readily self-sow.

■ **CULTIVATION AND CARE TIPS.** Plant chrysanthemums 12–18 in (30–45 cm) apart in full sun with humus-rich, well-drained soil. Double types of shasta daisy do better in light shade. The chrysanthemums discussed here are generally hardy to −30°F (−34°C), but the garden chrysanthemums vary greatly in hardiness. Many gardeners choose to buy or start new plants each year. Garden chrysanthemums transplant easily, so that plants in bud or full bloom can be set into the garden in the fall. If cuttings, seedlings, or divisions are set out in the spring, pinch out the growing tips of stems to six or eight leaves until mid-July; certain types, referred to as cushions, don't need pinching. Taller types must be staked. Deadhead regularly. Chrysanthemums benefit from a light summer mulch to keep soil moist and a winter mulch for protection.

■ **PROPAGATION.** Division of garden chrysanthemums in spring every year, painted daisies every fourth year, and shasta daisies every second or third year. Painted and shasta daisies and feverfew from seed. Cuttings taken in spring or summer.

■ **PESTS AND DISEASES.** Red spider mites; aphids; mildew; rust; verticillium wilt; mildew; yellows; leaf spot; borers; nematodes; leaf miners; rust. Species other than garden chrysanthemums are seldom bothered.

Chrysanthemum parthenium 'ULTRA DOUBLE WHITE'

Chrysogonum virginianum 'MARK VIETTE'

CHRYSOGONUM
GOLDEN STAR, GREEN-AND-GOLD

GOLDEN STAR (*C. virginianum*) grows 4–6 in (10–15 cm) tall with small, pointed leaves and delicate, star-shaped 1½-in (4-cm) golden yellow flowers. In mild climates, the leaves are evergreen. Leaves vary from smooth to hairy and dark green to gray-green.

■ **CULTIVATION AND CARE TIPS.** Growing best in light to full shade, the plants bloom all summer, especially in cooler climates or if the soil remains evenly moist but well-drained. Spreading by seed or rooting stems, golden star makes a good ground cover, edging, or accent in a shaded wildflower or rock garden; it does not become invasive. Set plants 12 in (30 cm) apart in humus-rich, moist but well-drained soil. Hardy to −20°F (−29°C).

■ **PROPAGATION.** Division in spring or fall.

■ **PESTS AND DISEASES.** Seldom bothered.

CIMICIFUGA
SNAKEROOT, BUGBANE

A GRACEFUL, DRAMATIC, low-maintenance plant for the back of a shady border, among shrubs, beside a pool or in open woodland, snakeroot produces large, open plants. Long, thin spires of white flowers arise in midsummer from the dark green, deeply cut and divided leaves. The seed spikes may be cut and dried for arrangements. Both may be used as fresh cut flowers as well.

■ **SPECIES, VARIETIES, AND CULTIVARS.** Black snakeroot, or black cohosh (*Cimicifuga racemosa*) grows to 6 ft (1.80 m) tall with creamy white flowers. The fall-blooming Kamchatka bugbane (*C. simplex*) has arching, white flowers, more finely textured foliage and grows 2–4 ft (60 cm–1.20 m) tall.

■ **CULTIVATION AND CARE TIPS.** Long-lived once established, they bloom best in light shade but tolerate both full shade or sun. They must have deep, moist, humus-rich, well-drained soil. Flower spikes may need staking. Set plants 2 ft (60 cm) apart with the rhizome 1 in (2.5 cm) deep. Be patient for plants to grow for several years before blooming. Hardy to −40°F (−40°C).

■ **PROPAGATION.** Division in spring, only if more plants are needed. Sow seed outdoors as soon as ripened.

■ **PESTS AND DISEASES.** Seldom bothered.

Cimicifuga racemosa

CLEMATIS

CLEMATIS

MOST OFTEN THOUGHT OF as vining plants, there are several shrubby perennial types that are easily grown and long lived. Clematis are unusual in that the flowers have no actual petals but rather petal-like sepals. Most types have plumed seeds almost as showy as the flowers. Both flowers and seed heads may be used in arrangements.

■ **SPECIES, VARIETIES, AND CULTIVARS.** Native to China, the tube clematis (*C. heracleifolia*) forms a mound 3 ft (90 cm) tall with coarse, broad, hairy leaves and spikes of fragrant blue flowers resembling hyacinths in late summer.

With sprawling growth, the solitary clematis (*C. integrifolia*) grows 2–4 ft (60 cm–1.20 m) tall with prominently veined leaves and 1-in (2.5-cm), bell-shaped lavender to violet-blue flowers in midsummer. A hybrid *C. × eriostemon* 'Hendersonii' is similar but with larger, indigo-blue flowers.

The ground clematis (*C. recta*) has slender twining stems growing 2–5 ft (60 cm–1.50 m) long and divided leaves. Plants are covered in masses of 1-in (2.5-cm) fragrant, star-shaped white flowers in early summer.

■ **CULTIVATION AND CARE TIPS.** Each of these clematis grows well in full sun to light shade and requires a humus-rich, moist but well-drained soil. A 2-in (5-cm) mulch of compost, or well-rotted manure, in summer will help to maintain the requisite cool soil. Care must be taken when cultivating around clematis as roots are easily damaged. Light staking is usually necessary, especially with ground clematis, or plants can be allowed to tumble over edges of raised beds, walls, or other plants. Trim back plants to 4–6 in (10–15 cm) tall in late fall or early spring. Set plants 18 in (45 cm) apart. Hardy to −30°F (−34°C).

■ **PROPAGATION.** Division in spring. Cuttings in summer.

■ **PESTS AND DISEASES.** Slugs; aphids; earwigs; borers; blister beetles; tarnished plant bugs; nematodes; powdery mildew; clematis wilt; leaf spot.

Clematis integrifolia 'COERULA'

Coreopsis verticillata 'MOONBEAM'

COREOPSIS

TICKSEED

THE SUNSHINE-YELLOW, daisy-like flowers of tickseed brighten borders and meadow gardens for much of the summer, especially if faded flowers are clipped off, or if the plants are cut back by one-third after the first flush of bloom. Very easily grown, the flowers are very long lasting when cut.

■ **SPECIES, VARIETIES, AND CULTIVARS.** The eared tickseed (*Coreopsis auriculata*) grows 1–2 ft (30–60 cm) tall with 1–2-in (2.5–5-cm) golden yellow flowers. The big-flowered tickseed (*C. grandiflora*) has narrow hairy leaves on 1–2 ft (30–60 cm) plants and 2–3-in (5–7.5-cm), long-stalked flowers. Very free-blooming and tolerant of dry soils, plants do not live long but readily self-sow. Lance tickseed (*C. lanceolata*) is similar, but it lives for a long time. Drought-tolerant and spreading slowly by underground stems, threadleaf tickseed

(*C. verticillata*) grows 12–30 in (30–75 cm) tall with very thin, thread-like leaves and masses of 2-in (5-cm) flowers.

■ **CULTIVATION AND CARE TIPS.** The species needs full sun, but both threadleaf and eared tickseed can tolerate light shade. Soil need only be average, but must be well-drained. Set plants 12 in (30 cm) apart. Hardy to −30°F (−34°C).

■ **PROPAGATION.** Division in spring every three or four years except for *C. grandiflora*, which is usually started from seed each year. All types can be started from seed.

■ **PESTS AND DISEASES.** Powdery mildew on all but threadleaf tickseed; leaf spot; rust; flea and striped cucumber beetles.

DELPHINIUM

LARKSPUR

CLASSIC PLANTS FOR the perennial border and one of the most spectacular but also one with pitfalls, larkspurs are known by their tall spikes of flowers, most often in shades of blue or purple. Plants grow 18 in–6 ft (45 cm–1.80 m) tall. They do best in cool, moist climates, but it is possible to grow them in other areas if expectations are lowered.

■ **SPECIES, VARIETIES, AND CULTIVARS.** Many hybrid varieties of candle larkspur (*D. elatum*) including doubles have been developed, growing to 6 ft (1.80 m). Each flower of these hybrids may be 1–3 in (2.5–7.5 cm) across, in shades of white, pink, lavender, blue, violet or purple. Remove all but three to five shoots in order to produce the largest stems and flowers.

Hybrid crosses of *D. elatum* and *D. grandiflorum* with some other species have yielded the popular 'Connect-icut Yankee' strain, growing 24–30 in (60–75 cm) tall with bushy, branching plants as well as the 'Bellamosa' and 'Belladonna' hybrids, growing 3–4 ft (90–120 cm) tall with a long blooming season.

The Chinese, or Siberian, larkspur (*D. grandiflorum*) is a short-lived perennial, often treated as an annual or biennial, but it flowers the first year from an early sowing. It grows 1–2 ft (30–60 cm) tall with finely divided leaves, branches freely, and bears open spikes of blue, purple, or white funnel-shaped, long-spurred flowers.

■ **CULTIVATION AND CARE TIPS.** They grow well in full sun to light shade and need a humus-rich, moist but well-drained, slightly alkaline soil. Mulching in the summer with several inches (cm) of compost or well-rotted manure keeps the roots cool and moist. Fertilize the plants in spring and again in early summer with 5–10–10. Use long enough stakes to go 12 in (30 cm) into the ground and reach two-thirds of the flower stem; tie at 12-in (30-cm) intervals. If possible, choose a site protected from strong winds. Space shorter types 12–18 in (30–45 cm) apart and taller ones 24–30 in (60–75 cm) apart. Cut faded flowering stems off just below the flower cluster to encourage reblooming. Cut all stems back to the ground in autumn. Hardy to −40°F (−40°C).

Delphinium HYBRIDS

■ **PROPAGATION.** Division in spring every third or fourth year. Basal cuttings in spring. Sow seed in late summer outdoors as soon as ripened or store in sealed plastic bags in the refrigerator and sow in early spring indoors or late spring outdoors.

■ **PESTS AND DISEASES.** Slugs; snails; mites; aphids; rot; powdery mildew; virus; leaf spot; botrytis.

DIANTHUS

CARNATION, PINKS

THE DELICIOUS, SPICY fragrance of carnations and pinks have made them prized for centuries, both in the garden and as cut flowers. The blooms are usually in shades of pink, red, or white, sometimes with a contrasting eye, a single five-petaled flower, a semi-double, or a double with many petals, and with the petals fringed or toothed. Most types have attractive dark or gray-green, grass-like foliage that forms mounds or mats. They adapt readily to rock gardens, walks, and walls, and are excellent for edgings. Easily hybridized, there are numerous cultivars and much confusion as to proper naming.

■ **SPECIES, VARIETIES, AND CULTIVARS.** The cottage pink, border carnation, or allwood pink (*Dianthus × allwoodii*) is a large, diverse group with many excellent varieties for the garden. The tufts of blue-green foliage grow 12 in (30 cm) tall and the flowers are like miniature carnations to 2 in (5 cm) across, single, semi-double, or double.

Wonderful for creating masses of color, sweet william (*D. barbatus*) is best treated as a short-lived perennial or biennial, but it readily self-sows so plants remain in the garden for many years. Growing 12–18 in (30–45 cm) tall with dark green leaves, the sturdy stems bear flat or rounded clusters 3–6 in (7.5–15 cm) across of numerous ½–1-in (12 mm–2.5 cm) flowers, which are often varicolored, but only lightly fragrant.

Dianthus deltoides 'ZING ROSE'

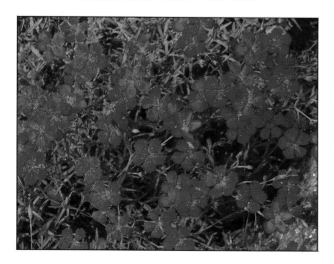

Dianthus plumarius

Maiden pink (*D. deltoides*) usually grows only 6 in (15 cm) tall, forming spreading mats of bright, semi-evergreen leaves. The early-summer, single flowers are less than 1 in (2.5 cm) across. Dainty cheddar pink (*D. gratianopolitanus*) forms neat, tidy mats of blue-gray leaves 6 in (15 cm) tall. Blooming mainly in early summer, some flowering continues until fall. The blooms are seldom more than ½-in (12 mm) across.

Cottage pink, grass pink, or Scotch pink (*D. plumarius*) forms loose mounds or mats of gray-green leaves 12 in (30 cm) or so tall. The 1–2-in (2.5–5-cm) flowers may be single, semi-double, or double and bloom over a long period.

The carnation (*D. caryophyllus*) is the flower purchased from florists. Although possible to grow in the garden, the other types of dianthus discussed are better suited.

■ **CULTIVATION, AND CARE TIPS.** Plants require full sun and do best in a sandy, humus-enriched well-drained, slightly alkaline soil. Poor drainage in winter is almost certain death, especially for low-growing types. They benefit from some loose winter protection, such as evergreen boughs, in colder areas. They are best treated as biennials in hot climates. Set plants 8–12 in (20–30 cm) apart. Deadhead regularly to prolong blooming or prevent self-seeding. Hardy to −30°F (−34°C).

■ **PROPAGATION.** Seed. Cuttings in summer. Division in spring.

■ **PESTS AND DISEASES.** Crown rot; spider mites; aphids; slugs; leaf spot.

Dicentra spectabilis

DICENTRA

BLEEDING HEART

ALL BLEEDING HEARTS are noted for their graceful shapes and unusually formed flowers, and are popular for cottage, rock and wildflower gardens. Most types are small-growing plants for the front of shaded beds or borders or a woodland garden, but one is taller and better suited to the middle of beds and borders. Bleeding hearts may self-sow but seldom become invasive.

■ **SPECIES, VARIETIES, AND CULTIVARS.** Dutchman's breeches (*Dicentra cucullaria*) and squirrel corn (*D. canadensis*) are early spring-blooming wildflowers with white flowers. With both, the fern-like, 10-in (25-cm) foliage dies back after blooming.

Much better suited for a lightly shaded perennial border are the fringed bleeding heart (*D. eximia*) and the Pacific, or western, bleeding heart (*D. formosa*). These form neat mounds 1 ft (30 cm) tall, with gray-green, feathery foliage and sprays of rose-pink, heart-shaped flowers from early spring until frost. The two species are difficult to distinguish.

Hybrids and cultivars of both species are available, including 'Bountiful', 'Zestful', and 'Luxuriant'. These are more tolerant of direct sun and have flowers in various shades of pink and red.

Common bleeding heart (*D. spectabilis*) forms a loose, open plant 2–3 ft (60–90 cm) tall, with divided leaves. In late spring, arching sprays of 1½-in (4-cm), rose-pink, heart-shaped flowers emerge. A pure white form is also available. Plants die back by midsummer, so they must be surrounded by other plants.

■ **CULTIVATION AND CARE TIPS.** They grow best with light to full shade in humus-rich, moist but well-drained soil. A summer mulch of compost or well-rotted manure will keep the soil cool and moist. Space the small-growing types 12 in (30 cm) apart and common bleeding heart 2 ft (60 cm) apart. Deadhead regularly to prolong blooming. Hardy to −40°F (−40°C).

■ **PROPAGATION.** Division in spring immediately after blooming, every three or four years. Seed. Root cuttings.

■ **PESTS AND DISEASES.** Seldom bothered.

Dictamnus alba 'PURPUREUS'

DICTAMNUS
GAS PLANT

A VERY LONG-LIVED, low-maintenance perennial, gas plant (*D. alba*, also called *D. fraxinella*) grows to a shrubby 2–3 ft (60–90 cm) tall with glossy, dark green leaves that remain attractive until frost. The common name comes from the volatile oils given off by the plant, and a match held to the flowers or seeds on a still summer evening will set off a flash of light. When crushed, the flowers and the foliage have the scent of lemons. Produced in numerous long spikes in early summer, the 1–2-in (2.5–5-cm) white blooms are good for cutting and are followed by interesting star-shaped seed pods useful in dried arrangements. Touching the flowers and seeds may cause an allergic reaction.

■ **CULTIVATION AND CARE TIPS.** It has deep roots, so does not transplant well and needs several years to become established, at which time it tolerates drought. Grow in full sun or very light shade with humus-rich, moist but well-drained soil. Set plants 3 ft (90 cm) apart. Hardy to −40°F (−40°C).

■ **PROPAGATION.** Seed sown outdoors in the fall sprout the following spring; seeds saved until the spring will germinate more readily if boiling water is poured over them. It may be three or four years before new plants bloom.

■ **PESTS AND DISEASES.** Seldom bothered.

DIGITALIS
FOXGLOVE

F OXGLOVE'S TALL SPIRES of velvety, dotted bells rising from low clumps of leaves provide a dramatic statement in the early summer garden. Use as a vertical accent in the middle to the back of a border, or let plants naturalize in an informal garden.

■ **SPECIES, VARIETIES, AND CULTIVARS.** Common foxglove (*Digitalis purpurea*) is a biennial growing 4 ft (1.20 m) or taller with 2-in (5-cm) flowers in white or shades of pink or purple; plants readily self-sow. The Merton hybrid foxgloves (*D. × mertonensis*) are perennials with pink, rose, or red flowers on spikes growing to 3 ft (90 cm) tall. The yellow foxglove (*D. grandiflora*, or *D. ambigua*) is a perennial with 2–3-in (5–7.5-cm) creamy yellow flowers dotted with brown on 3-ft (90-cm) stems. The straw foxglove (*D. lutea*) has white to pale yellow flowers on 1–2-ft (30–60-cm) spikes.

■ **CULTIVATION AND CARE TIPS.** They grow best in a humus-rich, moist but well-drained soil and full sun or partial shade. Remove faded flower stems if self-sowing is not desired; this may also encourage re-blooming. Set plants 12–18 in (30–45 cm) apart. Hardy to −30°F (−34°C). A winter mulch of evergreen boughs is helpful where there is little snow cover.

■ **PROPAGATION.** Division in spring after blooming. Seed sown outdoors in late summer for flowers the following year.

■ **PESTS AND DISEASES.** Leaf spot; mildew; rot; aphids; Japanese beetles; mealybugs.

Digitalis purpurea

Doronicum caucasicum

DORONICUM
LEOPARD'S BANE

GROWING 12–18 IN (30–45 cm) tall, the tidy, spreading mounds of glossy green, heart-shaped leaves make leopard's bane (*Doronicum caucasicum* also called *D. cordatum*) a good plant for the front of a border, a rock garden, or planted among spring bulbs and shrubs. In late spring or early summer the plants are covered with yellow, daisy-like 2-in (5-cm) flowers. They are long-lasting when cut but close at night. Leopard's bane goes dormant by late summer, so combine it with other plants that will fill in around it.

■ **CULTIVATION AND CARE TIPS.** They need humus-rich, moist but well-drained soil and either full sun or light shade. Set plants 12 in (30 cm) apart. Hardy to −30°F (−34°C).

■ **PROPAGATION.** Division every four years, in very early spring or late summer. Seed.

■ **PESTS AND DISEASES.** Mildew; aphids; Japanese beetles; mealybugs.

ECHINACEA
PURPLE CONEFLOWER

THIS LOW-MAINTENANCE, summer-blooming wild-flower is excellent when massed in informal plantings, or as a bold specimen in the middle or back of a border. Growing 2–4 ft (60 cm–1.20 m) tall, purple coneflowers have coarse, hairy stems and leaves and long-stalked, 4–6-in (10–15-cm) daisy-like flowers that bloom over a long period. The cone part, or center, of the flower is a brownish-orange and the rays, or petals, are magenta-pink and drooping. There are also white forms, plus other cultivars of various colors. The flowers attract butterflies, the blooms are good for cutting and the dried cones add texture to dried arrangements.

■ **CULTIVATION AND CARE TIPS.** Long-lived, the plants tolerate drought and grow well in a humus-rich, sandy soil that is well-drained; they tolerate either full sun or light shade. Staking is unnecessary except in very rich soil. Deadhead regularly to prolong blooming. Plant 18 in (45 cm) apart. Hardy to −40°F (−40°C).

■ **PROPAGATION.** Division every four years in early spring. Seed, but plants are variable.

■ **PESTS AND DISEASES.** Japanese beetles, mildew.

Echinacea purpurea

Echinops ritro

ECHINOPS
GLOBE THISTLE

AN UNUSUAL, EYE-CATCHING addition to the middle or back of flower beds or borders, as a specimen among shrubs, or in a meadow garden, globe thistles are also popular because they are good for arrangements, either fresh or dried. If drying, cut just before they open and hang upside down. The 1–2-in (2.5–5-cm) globe-like clusters of tiny, steel-blue flowers are borne on branching stems. Blooming for several months during summer, the flowers attract bees by day and moths at night. There is much confusion as to the scientific naming of this plant but most are sold as *Echinops ritro* or *E. humilis*. Plants grow 3–5 ft (90 cm–1.50 m) tall, with dark-green thistle-like leaves with a downy white underside.

■ **CULTIVATION AND CARE TIPS.** They are easily grown in full sun and almost any soil and tolerate heat and drought once established because of deep roots. Staking may be required if soil is rich. Set plants 18–24 in (45–60 cm) apart. Hardy to −30°F (−34°C).

■ **PROPAGATION.** Division in early spring, if necessary. Root cuttings. Seed, but plants are variable.

■ **PESTS AND DISEASES.** Japanese beetles; crown rot.

ERIGERON
FLEABANE

RESEMBLING ASTERS, with 2-in (5-cm) delicate, daisy-like flowers in shades of blue, pink, or white with yellow centers, fleabanes bloom during early and mid-summer. The flowers are excellent for cutting.

■ **SPECIES, VARIETIES, AND CULTIVARS.** A low-maintenance plant, the best fleabanes are the various hybrids, including lavender 'Azure Fairy', bright pink 'Forester's Darling', and pale pink 'Pink Jewel'. Plants are bushy and 18–30 in (45–75 cm) tall with shiny green leaves. Short types can be used in the rock garden. In the perennial garden, they are best when planted in groups of at least three; or allow to naturalize in a meadow garden, as plants readily self-sow.

■ **CULTIVATION AND CARE TIPS.** They do best in sandy, well-drained soil, and full sun in regions with cool summers but will withstand hotter temperatures with light shade. Set plants 12–18 in (30–45 cm) apart. Deadhead regularly. Hardy to −10°F (−23°C).

■ **PROPAGATION.** Division or basal cuttings in early spring. Seed.

■ **PESTS AND DISEASES.** Leaf spot; mildew; rust; aphids.

Erigeron

Eryngium HYBRID

ERYNGIUM

SEA HOLLY

A STRIKING, THISTLE-LIKE plant growing 2–4 ft (60 cm–1.20 m) tall, sea holly has prickly blue-gray foliage and white or purplish, 1-in (2.5-cm) cone-shaped flowers surrounded by a ruff of leaves. These branching stems of summer-blooming flowers are excellent for fresh or dried arrangements. Use the plants as an accent in the middle of flower beds and borders, in a rock garden, or a naturalized meadow garden.

■ **SPECIES, VARIETIES, AND CULTIVARS.** There is much disagreement over identification of sea hollies, and discrepancy among what plants are actually being sold. Amethyst sea holly (*Eryngium amethystinum*) grows 2 ft (60 cm) tall with white-veined leaves and blue-purple flowers; it is hardy to −40°F (−40°C). Flat-leaved sea holly (*E. planum*) grows 3 ft (90 cm) tall and has small blue flowers. True sea holly (*E. maritimum*) grows 12 in (30 cm) tall with white or pale blue flowers. Zabel's sea holly (*E.* × *zabelii*) grows 24–30 in (60–75 cm) tall with blue flowers. Bluetop sea holly (*E. alpinum*)

grows 2 ft (60 cm) tall; the flowers have a feathery blue ruff. The last two species are tolerant of clay soils and light shade. Giant sea holly (*E. giganteum*) is a biennial that grows 2–3 ft (60–90 cm) tall with greenish-white flowers. Mediterranean sea holly (*E. bourgatii*) grows 2 ft (60 cm) tall with white-veined leaves and slender white flower ruffs.

■ **CULTIVATION AND CARE TIPS.** They need sandy, well-drained soil and full sun. Long-lived, once planted they should not be disturbed. Deadhead to prevent self-sowing, unless desired. Set plants 12–24 in (30–60 cm) apart. Hardy to −20°F (−28°C).

■ **PROPAGATION.** Root cuttings, taken in spring only if absolutely necessary. Seed sown as soon as ripe will germinate the following spring; young plants transplant easily.

■ **PESTS AND DISEASES.** Leaf miner; beetles; rot; leaf spot.

Eupatorium purpureum

EUPATORIUM

MIST FLOWER, JOE-PYE WEED

BILLOWY CLUSTERS OF tiny flowers in shades of blue or pink during late summer and fall make these plants attractive in flower beds or borders and meadow gardens. Joe-Pye weed is especially effective naturalized in the damp soil beside streams and around marshes. Both mist flower and Joe-Pye weed attract butterflies and make good cut flowers.

■ **SPECIES, VARIETIES, AND CULTIVARS.** Mist flower, or hardy ageratum, (*Eupatorium coelestinum*) resembles the annual ageratum with its fluffy flowerheads of lavender-blue on 2-ft (60-cm) plants. The wrinkled leaves are thin and coarsely toothed. In sandy soil, plants may become invasive.

There are several species of eupatorium called Joe-Pye weed, including hollow Joe-Pye weed (*E. fistulosum*), hollow stems growing 6 ft (1.80 m) tall with rounded clusters of mauve flowers; spotted Joe-Pye weed (*E.*

maculatum), speckled stems growing to 10 ft (3 m) with loose, open clusters of purple flowers; and common Joe-Pye weed (*E. purpureum*), growing 6 ft (1.80 m) tall with large clusters of rose pink to purplish flowers.

■ **CULTIVATION AND CARE TIPS.** Both mist flower and Joe-Pye weed grow easily in full sun and a wide range of average to moist soils. Light shade is tolerated but plants bloom less. Set mist flower 18 in (45 cm) apart and Joe-Pye weed 3 ft (90 cm) apart. Mist flower is hardy to −20°F (−28°C) and Joe-Pye weed to −40°F (−40°C).

■ **PROPAGATION.** Division in spring, cuttings in summer, or seed. Mist flower needs dividing every two or three years.

■ **PESTS AND DISEASES.** Crown rot; blight; mildew; aphids; leaf miners; scales.

EUPHORBIA

SPURGE

ALTHOUGH THERE ARE over 1600 different spurges, only a few are of horticultural interest. Spurges are characterized by showy bracts, with very tiny flowers in the center. They have a milky sap, which can be a skin irritant.

■ **SPECIES, VARIETIES, AND CULTIVARS.** Cushion spurge (*E. epithymoides*, also called *E. polychroma*) forms an evenly rounded mound 12 in (30 cm) tall and 2 ft (60 cm) wide. The spring-blooming bracts are golden yellow, 1-in (2.5-cm) wide, and leaves turn rose-coloured in the fall. It may not do well in hot, humid climates.

E. griffithii 'Fire Glow' grows to 3 ft (90 cm) tall. The leaves have a pale pink midrib and the red bracts are in 2–4-in (5–10-cm) clusters during early summer. Because it easily tolerates dry soil, myrtle euphorbia (*E. myrsinites*) is a good choice for a rock garden or in a stone wall. A low, trailing plant, it is mainly grown for its blue-green leaves that remain on the plant year-round. The flowers are bright yellow in spring.

Resembling baby's breath, flowering spurge (*E. corollata*) grows 2 ft (60 cm) tall with loose clusters of tiny, showy white bracts in summer and are excellent for cutting. Sear cut stems in a candle flame to seal the end. Foliage turns red in the fall.

■ **CULTIVATION AND CARE TIPS.** Long-lived, these spurges grow best in full sun in dry, sandy soil. Light shade is beneficial in hot areas. Plants readily self-sow. Set plants 12–18 in (30–45 cm) apart. Hardy to −20°F (−28°C).

■ **PROPAGATION.** They do not transplant well, but if necessary, division in early spring. Seed. Cuttings.

■ **PESTS AND DISEASES.** Seldom bothered.

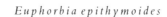

Euphorbia epithymoides

Athyrium felix-femina

FERNS

IMAGINE A LUSH, fern-filled glen on a hot summer's day and the usefulness of ferns in the garden is readily apparent. They are at their best when massed, especially under trees, along a wall, surrounding a pool, or on the north side of a house. They are very effective when combined with the early spring-flowering bulbs. The leaf form of a fern is called a frond, and ferns are reproduced by spores rather than seeds. The fronds are superb as foliage in flower arrangements.

■ **SPECIES, VARIETIES, AND CULTIVARS.** Considered one of the most beautiful ferns, maidenhair fern (*Adiantum pedatum*) has bright green, lacy fronds and black stems 12–18 in (30–45 cm) tall. Spreading slowly by rhizomes, it requires humus-rich, moist but well-drained soil and shade.

The lady fern (*Athyrium filix-femina*) grows in crowns with lacy fronds 2–3 ft (60–90 cm) tall. It tolerates a wide range of soils and grows in both sun or shade.

For drama in large areas, the ostrich fern (*Matteuccia pensylvanica*) with bright green, 4–6-ft (1.20–1.80-m) fronds is an effective ground cover. Spreading by rhizomes, it grows well in light shade and average soil or full sun if the soil is kept moist.

Sensitive fern (*Onoclea sensibilis*) has unusual gray-green fronds growing 2 ft (60 cm) tall and stalks with spore-bearing "pods" prized for flower arrangements. It readily spreads by rhizomes in sun or shade and moist garden soil.

The cinnamon fern (*Osmunda cinnamomea*) grows 4–6 ft (1.20–1.80 m) tall with pale green fronds turning golden, then brown in the fall. Tolerating average garden soil, this crown-spreading fern grows the biggest in moist soil in full sun or light shade.

The royal fern (*O. regalis*) grows 4–6 ft (1.20–1.80 m) tall with dramatic fronds that are unusual in that there are fertile flower-like spikes at the tips of some. Constantly moist, acidic soil and shade is necessary. Plants spread slowly from crowns.

The dainty evergreen common polypody (*Polypodium virginianum*) spreads by rhizomes over rocks and fallen trees with 6–10-in (15–25-cm) leathery fronds. A wide range of conditions is tolerated but best growth is with moist but well-drained soil and light shade.

Related to the Boston fern, the evergreen Christmas fern (*Polystichum acroistichoides*) is one of the easiest ferns to grow. Tolerant of a wide range of conditions, light shade and humus-rich, moist but well-drained soil is ideal. It spreads slowly by rhizomes.

■ **CULTIVATION AND CARE TIPS.** In general, they grow best in a shady location with humus-rich, loose soil that is moist but well-drained and a light mulch of compost, bark, or shredded leaves. Set plants 12–30 in (30–75 cm) apart. Hardy to −40°F (−40°C).

■ **PROPAGATION.** Division of creeping types at any time and ones with crowns when dormant in early spring or late fall.

■ **PESTS AND DISEASES.** Some ferns may be bothered by slugs and snails.

Osmunda cinnamomea

Filipendula vulgaris 'FLORE-PLENO'

FILIPENDULA

QUEEN-OF-THE-PRAIRIE, QUEEN-OF-THE-MEADOW, DROPWORT

THE PLUMY CLUSTERS OF tiny pink or white flowers and the lush, dark green, compound leaves of these plants make them a source of fine texture in the garden. The flowers are good for cutting, if picked before they are fully open.

■ **SPECIES, VARIETIES, AND CULTIVARS.** Queen-of-the-prairie (*F. rubra*) sends up numerous stalks 4–7 ft (1.20–2.10 m) tall with clusters of rosy pink, fragrant flowers at the tips in mid-summer. Queen-of-the-meadow (*F. ulmaria*) has fragrant, white flower clusters in early summer on 3–5-ft (90-cm–1.50-m) plants. Use these two plants in the back of a border, planted among shrubs, or beside a stream. Dropwort (*F. vulgaris*, also called *F. hexapetala*) has fern-like leaves in a ground-hugging clump and ivory flowers on 18–24-in (45–60 cm) stalks in early summer; it readily self-sows. Plant at the front of a border or in a woodland garden.

■ **CULTIVATION AND CARE TIPS.** Provide a humus-rich, moist but well-drained soil; dropwort tolerates some dryness. Plants do best in light shade, but grow in full sun in cooler, northern climates. Set queen-of-the-meadow and queen-of-the-prairie 2 ft (60 cm) apart and dropwort 12 in (30 cm) apart. Hardy to −40°F (−40°C). If there is no snow cover in cold areas, mulch with leaves to protect the roots.

■ **PROPAGATION.** Division in spring. Seed.

■ **PESTS AND DISEASES.** Mildew, if plants are grown in soil too dry.

Galium odoratum

GAILLARDIA

BLANKETFLOWER

BLANKETFLOWERS READILY PRODUCE brightly colored, daisy-like 3–4-in (7.5–10-cm) blooms for much of the summer. The flowers are various combinations of yellow, gold, and red, often with purple centers. The taller-growing types are good for cutting.

■ **SPECIES, VARIETIES, AND CULTIVARS.** The common perennial blanketflower (*G. aristata*) is a sprawling 2–3-ft (60–90-cm) plant with gray-green, hairy leaves. Excellent for the meadow or wild garden, it is one of the main parents of many popular hybrids.

■ **CULTIVATION AND CARE TIPS.** They tend to be short-lived in fertile, moist soils, but last longer with full sun in average to poor, very well-drained soil, especially in winter. Deadhead and trim back plants in late summer for more bloom in the fall. If plants do not bloom, divide them in early spring. Set plants 6–18 in (15–45 cm) apart. Hardy to −40°F (−40°C).

■ **PROPAGATION.** Division in early spring. Basal cuttings in late summer or root cuttings in fall and overwintered in a coldframe. Seed.

■ **PESTS AND DISEASES.** Leaf spot; powdery mildew; aster yellow; beetles; leafhoppers; sowbugs.

Gaillardia HYBRID

GALIUM

SWEET WOODRUFF

A LOW-MAINTENANCE ground cover for shaded areas, sweet woodruff (*G. odoratum*, also known as *Asperula odorata*) is used fresh as an herb. The dried leaves are used to flavour liqueurs and scent insect-repelling sachets. Small, star-shaped fragrant white flowers are scattered across the tops of the 6–8-in (15–20-cm) mounds of thin, whorled leaves in spring and early summer.

■ **CULTIVATION AND CARE TIPS.** It prefers partial shade in moist but well-drained, humus-rich soil. Plant 12 in (30 cm) apart. Hardy to −30°F (−34°C).

■ **PROPAGATION.** Division in spring or fall, as desired, although seldom required.

■ **PESTS AND DISEASES.** Seldom bothered.

GERANIUM

CRANESBILL

TRUE GERANIUMS, not the summer bedding plants that are the genus *Pelargonium*, are lovely perennials with delicate 1–2-in (2.5–5-cm) pastel flowers often borne all summer long. There are many different geraniums for the garden, with most growing as compact or open mounds. The attractive foliage is rounded and usually finely divided and toothed. Geraniums are best used toward the front of a border or along paths.

■ **SPECIES, VARIETIES, AND CULTIVARS.** G. × *cantabrigiense* forms a 6–12-in (15–30-cm), slowly spreading mat of scented green leaves. Bright rose-pink flowers bloom in late spring and occasionally through the summer.

G. *endressii* 'Wargrave Pink' grows 2 ft (60 cm) tall and spreads to 3 ft (90 cm). The warm-pink, 1½-in (4-cm) flowers are borne throughout summer in cool climates and for a shorter period in hotter areas unless soil is kept evenly moist.

The lilac cranesbill is G. *himalayense*, but it may also be listed as G. *grandiflorum* or G. *meeboldii*. Spreading mounds combine with 2-in (5-cm) blue flowers with purple veins. Bigroot cranesbill (G. *macrorrhizum*) makes an aromatic ground cover growing 12–18 in (30–45 cm) tall. In late spring and early summer, plants produce dense clusters of 1-in (2.5-cm) pink, magenta, or white flowers.

G. *maculatum* has loose, open growth to 2 ft (60 cm) tall and pink flowers in spring. It is good for lightly shaded wildflower gardens. G. × *oxonianum* 'Claridge Druce' forms a broad mound 2 ft (60 cm) tall with gray-green leaves and 2-in (5-cm) trumpet-shaped pink flowers with darker veins.

Blood-red cranesbill (G. *sanguineum*) forms a mound 12–18 in (30–45 cm) tall with long-blooming, 1-in (2.5-cm), pink to magenta flowers. It is highly adaptable to various climates and also self-sows readily. If soil is too rich, it will spread excessively. Foliage turns deep red in autumn.

Two species are very good for the rock garden, G. *cinereum* and G. *dalmaticum*. Both grow 4–6 in (10–15 cm) tall, with lilac, magenta, pink or white flowers.

■ **CULTIVATION AND CARE TIPS.** They bloom best in full sun, but in hotter climates plants grow better with light shade. Average, moist but well-drained soil is best; overly rich soil encourages rampant growth. Set plants 12 in (30 cm) apart. Hardy to −30°F (−34°C).

■ **PROPAGATION.** Division in spring every four years or when clumps begin to deteriorate. Seed for species. Cuttings in summer.

■ **PESTS AND DISEASES.** Leaf spot; mildew; rust; plant bugs.

Geranium 'JOHNSON'S BLUE'

Geum 'MRS BRADSHAW'

GEUM

GEUM, AVENS

GEUMS FORM LOW CLUMPS of dark green leaves with thin, branching stems bearing 1½-in (4-cm) red, yellow, or orange flowers with wavy petals during summer. Lower-growing types are good in rock gardens; the taller ones (good for cutting) are best used toward the front of beds and borders.

■ **SPECIES, VARIETIES, AND CULTIVARS.** *G. rivale* 'Leonard's Variety' grows 12 in (30 cm) tall and has copper-rose, bell-shaped flowers on red stems. It must have moist soil and light shade. Hardy to −40°F (−40°C). There are a number of hybrid cultivars of the taller type, and most grow 18–24 in (45–60 cm) tall.

■ **CULTIVATION AND CARE TIPS.** They grow best in full sun in cool-summer areas, but light shade is preferable in hot climates. Soil must be humus-rich and moist but well-drained. Soggy soil in winter is fatal. Plants are slow to become established, and the varieties listed will not need dividing for many years. Set plants 12–18 in (30–45 cm) apart; they are best in groups of three. Deadhead regularly to prolong blooming. The taller hybrids are hardy to −20°F (−28°C) with a loose winter mulch.

■ **PROPAGATION.** Division in spring or late summer.

■ **PESTS AND DISEASES.** Sowbugs and spider mites.

GYPSOPHILA

BABY'S BREATH

THE BILLOWING CLOUDS of tiny white or pink flowers of baby's breath provide a fine-textured addition to the flower garden as well as to both fresh and dried bouquets. The thin, wiry, branching stems have a few narrow, gray-green leaves.

■ **SPECIES, VARIETIES, AND CULTIVARS.** Long-lived *G. paniculata* grows 18–36 in (45–90 cm) tall, depending on the variety, from thick, fleshy taproots that do not transplant well. The sprays of ¼-in (6-mm) flowers are produced during summer. Plants may become top-heavy and should be staked early in the season. With a long growing season, a second bloom is possible by trimming plants back after the first one. Creeping baby's breath (*G. reptans*) grows 4–12 in (10–30 cm) tall with masses of whitish-pink flowers. This is best in rock gardens or spilling over walls.

■ **CULTIVATION AND CARE TIPS.** It grows in full sun with average, well-drained, alkaline soil. Plant 1–2 ft (30–60 cm) apart, in early spring. Many named varieties are grafted; set the graft union 1–2 in (2.5–5 cm) below the soil. Hardy to −30°F (−34°C), applying a loose mulch in winter after the ground is frozen.

■ **PROPAGATION.** The best kinds are purchased as grafted plants. Ordinary forms are grown from seeds or cuttings.

■ **PESTS AND DISEASES.** Botrytis; crown gall; yellows; leafhoppers.

Gypsophila paniculata 'COMPACTA-PLENA'

Helenium hoopesii

HELENIUM
SNEEZEWEED

LARGE PLANTS FOR THE middle to back of informal borders, in meadows or planted among shrubs, sneezeweed provides bright colors in the summer and fall. Daisy-like flowers with drooping yellow, orange, or mahogany petals and prominent dark centers are borne profusely in branching clusters. The flowers are good for cutting, and plants are long-lived and never invasive.

■ **SPECIES, VARIETIES, AND CULTIVARS.** Common sneezeweed, or false sunflower (*H. autumnale*) grows 6 feet (1.80 m) tall with each flower 2 in (5 cm) wide. Orange sneezeweed (*H. hoopesii*) grows 2 ft (60 cm) tall and blooms in early summer with large yellow-orange or gold flowers. It tolerates light shade.

■ **CULTIVATION AND CARE TIPS.** It grows well in full sun with a moist but well-drained, humus-rich soil, but tolerates a range of soils. Pinch out growing tips of taller-growing types in spring to make plants shorter and bushier. Provide staking for support. Set 18–24 in (45–60 cm) apart. Hardy to −40°F (−40°C).

■ **PROPAGATION.** Division in spring every two or three years. Cuttings. Species from seed.

■ **PESTS AND DISEASES.** Rust; leaf spot; mildew; beetles.

HELIOPSIS
FALSE SUNFLOWER

VIGOROUS, BOLD PLANTS with dark green foliage, false sunflowers have abundant clusters of golden, daisy-like flowers 2–4 in (5–10 cm) across, with slightly darker centers, blooming from summer through fall. The species is best planted in an area where it can naturalize by self-sowing. Hybrid cultivars are also good at the back of flower borders, the center of beds, or planted among shrubs. Cut flowers are long-lasting.

Heliopsis helianthoides varies in the wild, but is generally 5 ft (1.50 m) tall. Hybrids are usually shorter, growing 2–3 ft (60–90 cm) tall.

■ **CULTIVATION AND CARE TIPS.** Although drought-tolerant, they grow best in full sun with average to humus-rich, moist but well-drained soil. Deadhead regularly to prolong blooming. Set plants 2 ft (60 cm) apart. Hardy to −30°F (−34°C).

■ **PROPAGATION.** Division in early spring every three or four years. Seed in spring or summer.

■ **PESTS AND DISEASES.** Aphids; beetles; leaf spot; mildew; stem rot.

Heliopsis helianthoides

Helleborus orientalis

HELLEBORUS

HELLEBORE

ALTHOUGH NOT ALWAYS as early-blooming as advertised, hellebores are still among the earliest perennials to flower, with blooming time varying from midwinter to spring, depending on the climate. Lasting a month or more, the nodding flowers are able to withstand cold temperatures and snow. Totally unrelated to roses, the flowers have five petal-like sepals and prominent golden stamens in the center. Hellebores have long-stemmed, segmented leaves growing 12–18 in (30–45 cm) tall and may self-sow but are never invasive. Choose a site where they can be enjoyed at close range, such as near a doorway. They are good for cutting, if stem ends are seared in a flame immediately. Plants may cause an allergic reaction in some people.

■ **SPECIES, VARIETIES, AND CULTIVARS.** Christmas rose (*Helleborus niger*) grows 12 in (30 cm) tall with 2–4-in (5–10 cm) white flowers tinged with pink or green, blooming from midwinter to early spring, one to three to a stem. Foliage is thick, evergreen, and saw-toothed. Hardy to −40°F (−40°C). Lenten rose (*H. orientalis*) blooms from late winter through spring with 2-in (5-cm) flowers that may be cream, purple-pink, maroon-brown, or greenish-white, sometimes with rose-purple spots. This 18-in (45 cm) tall species hybridizes readily and there are many forms, all of which are among the easiest to grow of the hellebores. Hardy to −30°F (−34°C).

Corsican hellebore (*H. argutifolius*, also listed as *H. corsicus* or *H. lividus corsicus*) has large clusters of pale green 1-in (2.5-cm) flowers in early spring on leafy stems 1–2 ft (30–60 cm) tall. Hardy to −20°F (−28°C). Stinking hellebore (*H. foetidus*) has clusters of pale green 1-in (2.5-cm) flowers, rimmed in purple as they age, on leafy stems 12–18 in (30–45 cm) tall. Hardy to −40°F (−40°C).

■ **CULTIVATION AND CARE TIPS.** Ideally, they need sun in the winter and shade in the summer with a humus-rich, neutral, moist but well-drained soil. Planting under deciduous trees or among other perennials are ways of achieving this. Do not allow soil to dry out in summer; a mulch is beneficial. Set plants 18 in (45 cm) apart with the crown 1 in (2.5 cm) below the soil line and allow several years for the long-lived plants to become established before they bloom well. Winter protection of various types may be used, including mulching loosely with oak leaves or pine boughs or building a plastic-covered frame to set over plants.

■ **PROPAGATION.** Division of the roots in spring after flowering or in fall is possible but not recommended. Seed sown as soon as ripened.

■ **PESTS AND DISEASES.** Slugs; leaf spot; mildew; rot.

Helleborus argutifolius

Hemerocallis 'STELLA D'OR'

HEMEROCALLIS

DAY LILY

EASILY GROWN AND widely adaptable, day lilies have become among the most popular of all perennial plants, with thousands of different hybrid varieties. For a long period during summer, leafless stalks rise from the thick clumps of arching, grassy leaves and bear open clusters of lily-like, sometimes fragrant, flowers. Each flower lasts only a day, but a plant may produce dozens during a season.

Depending on the height, day lilies may be used at the front, middle, back or center of flower beds and borders. Smaller types are good in rock gardens. Day lilies are also quite effective as an edging, grown among shrubs, or massed in an informal setting.

■ **SPECIES, VARIETIES, AND CULTIVARS.** The original species have yellow or orange flowers, but the colors of the hybrid cultivars are extremely varied, often with a contrasting stripe, edge, or throat. Most have six petals, but some are doubles, and petals may be frilled or ruffled. The size of the plants in bloom varies from 12 in (30 cm) to over 6 ft (1.80 m) and flower size from 2–8 in (5–20 cm) across. Depending on the cultivar, bloom time can be late spring, summer, or fall, and some types bloom repeatedly.

■ **CULTIVATION AND CARE TIPS.** They thrive in sun or light shade. Although a wide range of soil is tolerated, best growth is with a humus-rich, moist but well-drained soil. Extra watering during hot weather is recommended, but too much fertilizer will force plants into excessive growth at the cost of bloom. Specimen plants should be deadheaded; this is impossible with massed plantings. Set shorter types 12–18 in (30–45 cm) apart and larger ones 2 ft (60 cm) apart. Types that go dormant are hardy to −30°F (−34°C); evergreen and semi-evergreen types vary in hardiness and are best in warmer climates.

■ **PROPAGATION.** Division of clumps of rhizomatous roots in late summer or fall, with clumps usually becoming overcrowded after about four to six years. Plantlets that develop on flower stalks can be removed and rooted.

■ **PESTS AND DISEASES.** Aphids; thrips; spider mites; slugs.

HESPERIS

SWEET ROCKET, DAME'S ROCKET

SWEET ROCKET (*H. matronalis*) is a lovely, cottage garden plant, resembling phlox, with wonderfully fragrant elongated clusters of lavender, purple, mauve or white ½-in (12-mm) flowers from late spring to midsummer. Good for cut flowers, sweet rocket is short-lived as a perennial, but self-sows readily. The bushy plants grow 2–3 ft (60–90 cm) tall and can be used in the flower border or in meadow gardens.

■ **CULTIVATION AND CARE TIPS.** It thrives best in full sun or partial shade with moist but well-drained alkaline soil. Set plants 18 in (45 cm) apart. Deadhead regularly to prolong blooming. Hardy to −40°F (−40°C).

■ **PROPAGATION.** Seeds

■ **PESTS AND DISEASES.** Mildew; rust; mosaic spread by aphids; cabbage worms.

Hesperis matronalis

Heuchera sanguinea 'CHATTERBOX'

HEUCHERA

CORAL BELLS

CORAL BELLS (*Heuchera sanguinea*) give a light, airy touch when planted in a rock garden, at the front of a flower bed, among shrubs, or as an edging to a path. From late spring through summer, wiry stems of tiny pink, red, or white bell-shaped flowers emerge from the low-growing clumps of rounded, mottled leaves that are evergreen in mild climates. The long-lasting flowers are good for cutting. The clumps grow 6–10 in (15–25 cm) tall and the flower stalks 1–2 ft (30–60 cm) tall. There are a number of excellent hybrid cultivars available.

■ **CULTIVATION AND CARE TIPS.** They grow best with a humus-rich, moist but well-drained soil. Good drainage in winter is essential. Choose a site with full sun or light shade, with the latter preferable in hot, dry climates. Space plants 12 in (30 cm) apart and set crowns 1 in (2.5 cm) deep in spring. Deadhead regularly to prolong blooming. Hardy to −40°F (−40°C). Mulch with evergreen boughs after the ground has frozen to prevent winter heaving of roots.

■ **PROPAGATION.** Division in spring or fall, usually every three to five years, or when the crown becomes woody. Younger plants can be divided for increase.

■ **PESTS AND DISEASES.** Root weevils; mealybugs; stem rot.

Hibiscus moscheutos HYBRID

HIBISCUS

ROSE MALLOW, HIBISCUS

EXOTIC AND BOLD, rose mallow (*H. moscheutos*) makes a dramatic statement in the garden with the 6–12-in (15–30-cm) saucer-shaped flowers on 3–6-ft (90-cm–1.80-m) plants with broad leaves. Blooming from midsummer to fall, the flowers may be white or shades of pink or red. Use as a specimen plant or accent in flower beds or among shrubs. A number of hybrid cultivars are also available. Scarlet rose mallow (*H. coccineus*) grows 6–8 ft (1.80–2.40 m) tall with fine-textured blue-green leaves and 6-in (15-cm) crimson flowers. It is best for naturalizing.

■ **CULTIVATION AND CARE TIPS.** They grow best in full sun with humus-rich, moist soil. Light shade and drier soil are tolerated once plants are established. Long-lived and resenting disturbance, they are also slow to sprout in the spring. Set plants 3 ft (90 cm) apart. Hardy to −20°F (−28°C), but in areas with a low of 0°F (−18°C) or less, a winter mulch is desirable.

■ **PROPAGATION.** Although seldom necessary, division in spring, setting the leaf buds 4 in (10 cm) deep. Cuttings. Seed.

■ **PESTS AND DISEASES.** Leaf spot; gall; rust; stem rot; aphids; Japanese beetles; scales; white flies.

PLANTAIN LILY, FUNKIA

ONE OF THE MOST POPULAR and widely used of perennials, plantain lilies are chosen for their adaptability to various climates and soils, low-maintenance and the attractiveness of the neat, symmetrical mounds of leaves of varying textures and colors. Besides the numerous species, thousands of hybrid cultivars have been developed, ranging in size from less than 6 in (15 cm) to over 3 ft (90 cm) across, and often with variegated leaves. Although plantain lilies have spikes of white, purple, or lavender flowers in summer or fall, some of which are fragrant, they are mainly grown as foliage plants. Use plantain lilies as specimens or in small groups in beds or borders, edging walks, or massed as a ground cover.

Hostas

■ **SPECIES, VARIETIES, AND CULTIVARS.** Blunt-leaf plantain lily (*H. decorata*, also listed as 'Thomas Hogg') grows 2 ft (60 cm) tall with 6-in (15-cm) leaves rimmed in white and dark lavender flowers in August. Fortune's plantain lily (*H. fortunei*) grows 2 ft (60 cm) tall, with 5–8-in (12.5–20-cm) heart-shaped, gray-green leaves and lavender flowers in midsummer.

Narrow plantain lily (*H. lancifolia*) grows 2 ft (60 cm) tall and as wide with narrow, glossy, dark green leaves 4–6 in (1–15 cm) long and white-violet flowers in late summer and early fall.

Fragrant plantain lily (*H. plantaginea*) is an old-fashioned favorite with large, fragrant white flowers in late summer, 10-in (25-cm), heart-shaped leaves forming plants 3 ft (90 cm) wide.

Siebold's plantain lily (*H. sieboldiana*) grows 30 in (75 cm) tall and twice as wide with 10–15-in (25–38-cm) long heart-shaped, blue-green puckered leaves and lavender flowers on short, partly hidden stalks bloom in summer.

Autumn plantain lily (*H. tardifolia*) grows 12 in (30 cm) tall with narrow, dark green leaves and deep purple flowers in late autumn. Wavy-leaf plantain lily (*H. undulata*) has pointed leaves 6 in (15 cm) long striped in white or cream with lavender flowers on 3 ft (90 cm) stalks in midsummer.

Blue plantain lily (*H. ventricosa*) has large glossy, dark green heart-shaped leaves and tall spikes of purple flowers in late summer and early fall.

■ **CULTIVATION AND CARE TIPS.** They do best in light to deep shade and humus-rich, moist but well-drained soil. Wet soil in winter is very detrimental. Full sun is tolerated if soil is kept moist during the growing season, but variegated types may be less colorful. Remove faded bloom stalks from plantings when feasible. Set plants 1–2 ft (30–60 cm) apart, depending on mature size. Hardy to −30°F (−34°C).

■ **PROPAGATION.** Division of young plants in spring for increase only, otherwise leave undisturbed.

■ **PESTS AND DISEASES.** Slugs; snails; crown rot in wet soils.

CANDYTUFT

ONE OF THE BEST spring-blooming plants, the 2-in (5-cm) clusters of white blooms of candytuft (*I. sempervirens*) are set off by the dense, fine-textured, dark evergreen leaves on creeping woody plants 6–10 in (15–25 cm) tall and 2 ft (60 cm) wide. It is excellent in a rock garden, tumbling over walls, at the front of beds and borders, as an edging, or in planters. There are a number of cultivars available.

■ **CULTIVATION AND CARE TIPS.** It grows best in full sun with a humus-rich, neutral to alkaline, moist but well-drained soil. Prune stems back halfway after flowering to keep the plant bushy. Once well-established, leave undisturbed and it will be long-lived. Set plants 15 in (38 cm) apart. Hardy to −30°F (−34°C).

■ **PROPAGATION.** Cuttings in early summer. Divisions in early summer after flowering.

■ **PESTS AND DISEASES.** Club root; mildew; rust; caterpillars; scales.

Iberis sempervirens

IRIS

IRIS

THOUSANDS OF VARIETIES in almost every color except red, coupled with the sheer beauty of the unusually-shaped blooms, have made irises a garden favorite for centuries. Flowers consist of three upright petals called standards and three drooping petals called falls. Flowers may be bicolored, and petals may be frilled, ruffled, or edged in a different color; a crest or beard may decorate the center of the falls. Flowering is usually in spring or summer, with a few cultivars of the tall bearded iris repeat-blooming in the fall. Foliage is narrow, stiff, and sword-shaped, and plants grow by spreading, fleshy, rhizomatous roots. Use the shorter irises in a rock garden or at the front of flower beds and borders. Japanese irises are ideal planted at the edge of streams or in other moist areas. Taller irises can be planted in the middle to back of flower beds and borders, along a wall, or among shrubs. Irises are superb cut flowers.

■ **SPECIES, VARIETIES, AND CULTIVARS.** The most familiar irises are the bearded hybrids (often grouped under the heading *Iris germanica*), which are divided into dwarf, intermediate and tall classes, with further subdivisions according to flower size. Height ranges from 8 to 30 in (20 to 75 cm) and flowers from 1½ to 8 in (4 to 20 cm).

The long-lived Siberian iris (*I. sibirica*) is the easiest one to grow. Plants reach 3 ft (90 cm) tall with graceful, slender leaves and 3-in (7.5-cm) flowers in shades of white, blue, purple, red-purple, and violet. They bloom in summer after the bearded irises. Scatter clumps throughout flower beds and borders, as they tolerate

Iris ensata 'ELEANOR PARRY'

Iris sibirica

both full sun and light shade. Leave seed pods on the plants or cut for dried arrangements.

Japanese iris (*I. ensata*) grows 3–4 ft (90 cm–1.20 m) tall with flat, 6-in (15-cm) flowers in shades of white, blue, rose and purple in midsummer.

Crested iris (*I. cristata*) is one of the smaller irises, growing just 6 in (15 cm) tall with pale lavender-blue or white flowers in spring.

Roof iris (*I. tectorum*) grows 8–12 in (20–30 cm) tall with lavender-blue or white 3-in (7.5-cm) flowers. It grows in both full sun and light shade.

■ **CULTIVATION AND CARE TIPS.** Unless otherwise noted, they grow best in full sun but tolerate light shade. Bearded, crested, Siberian, and roof irises need a humus-rich, moist but well-drained soil with the rhizomes 1 in (2.5 cm) below the soil surface. Japanese irises prefer humus-rich, constantly moist soils. Siberian and roof irises do best with slightly acid soil. Except as noted, deadhead regularly. Set shorter types 12 in (30 cm) apart and taller types 18 in (45 cm) apart. Hardy to −20°F (−28°C).

■ **PROPAGATION.** Division of rhizomes after flowering. Bearded iris usually need dividing every three or four years.

■ **PESTS AND DISEASES.** Iris borer followed by bacterial soft rot, evidenced by trails of slime along leaf edges. Begin spraying in spring and repeat weekly for three weeks; remove and destroy infected rhizomes at any time and old foliage and litter in the fall to prevent overwintering borer eggs.

KNIPHOFIA

TORCH LILY, RED-HOT POKER

DENSE MOUNDS OF gracefully arching gray-green leaves yield stiff spikes of bright orange, red, cream, coral, or yellow flowers for a long period in summer. The hybrids bloom in midsummer and the species in late summer and early fall. Foliage grows 12–30 in (30–75 cm) tall and the flower spikes reach 2–4 ft (60 cm–1.20 m) tall.

Torch lilies are long lived and are best used as individual accent plants or in groups of three in the front to middle of flower beds and borders. The flowers are good for cutting and attract humming birds.

■ **SPECIES, VARIETIES, AND CULTIVARS.** The species (*K. uvaria*, also listed as *K. pfitzeri* or *Tritoma uvaria*) is hardy to 0°F (−18°C), but the various hybrid cultivars are hardy to −20°F (−28°C), especially with a loose winter mulch of evergreen boughs or leaves.

■ **CULTIVATION AND CARE TIPS.** They grow well in full sun with humus-rich, moist but well-drained soil. Wet soil in winter is usually fatal. Avoid windy sites as plants are difficult to stake. Set plants 18 in (45 cm) apart, planting in spring.

■ **PROPAGATION.** Division in early spring every four or five years, if desired, removing young side growths or digging the entire plant and separating.

■ **PESTS AND DISEASES.** Leaf spot; nematodes.

Kniphofia HYBRID

Lavandula angustifolia

LAVANDULA

LAVENDER

AN OLD-FASHIONED garden favorite, lavender is beloved for the scent of its flowers and leaves as well as for its effectiveness as a specimen plant in beds, borders, and rock gardens, and as an edging or low hedge. Needle-like, gray-green leaves and lavender, purple, pink, or white flowers provide a fine-textured, softly blending plant for the garden. Flowers are produced from early to late summer, and they can be used in fresh arrangements or dried for use in potpourri and sachets. Lavender (*L. angustifolia*, also listed as *L. officinalis, L. vera*, or *L. spica*) grows 1–3 ft (30–90 cm) tall.

■ **CULTIVATION AND CARE TIPS.** It needs full sun and sandy, alkaline, well-drained soil that is not too fertile. Prune back old wood in the spring. Set plants 12 in (30 cm) apart. Hardy to −20°F (−28°C). A winter mulch in climates of 0°F (−18°C) or colder is necessary.

■ **PROPAGATION.** Cuttings in early summer. Seed.

■ **PESTS AND DISEASES.** Seldom bothered.

LIATRIS
GAYFEATHER, BLAZING STAR

TALL, NARROW WANDS of purple, magenta, or white small, fluffy flowers, excellent for attracting butterflies, bloom from midsummer to early fall. Superb for cutting and using fresh or dried, the flowers are unusual in that they open from the top downward. The stiff, narrow, dark green foliage forms grassy tufts that have a fine-textured appearance. Utilize the strong vertical effect of gayfeather toward the middle of flower beds and borders or in meadow gardens.

■ **SPECIES, VARIETIES, AND CULTIVARS.** Kansas gayfeather (*L. pycnostachya*) grows 4–5 ft (1.20–1.50 m) tall with 1-in (2.5-cm) rosy-lavender flowers in late summer and early fall. Spiked gayfeather (*L. spicata*) has stems densely covered with leaves and deep magenta or white ½-in (12-mm) flowers in summer. Plants grow 3 ft (90 cm) tall.

■ **CULTIVATION AND CARE TIPS.** Long-lived, they grow well in full sun with sandy to average, moist but well-drained soils. Tolerant of dry soil, they must have good winter drainage. Staking may be required. Deadhead to prevent self-sowing. Set plants 12–18 in (30–45 cm) apart. Hardy to −40°F (−40°C).

■ **PROPAGATION.** Division of crowded plants every three or four years in early spring. Seed.

■ **PESTS AND DISEASES.** Seldom bothered.

Liatris spicata

Linum perenne

LINUM
FLAX

PERENNIAL FLAX FORMS graceful, upright clumps with small, fine-textured leaves and delicate-looking flowers of blue, yellow, or white. Each bloom lasts only a day, but if kept picked, plants bloom all summer. Use flax in the front or middle of beds, borders and in rock gardens. Blue flax is also good in meadow gardens.

■ **SPECIES, VARIETIES, AND CULTIVARS.** Blue flax (*L. perenne*) grows 18–24 in (45–60 cm) tall with blue-green leaves and clear-blue or white 1-in (2.5-cm) flowers. Narbonne flax (*L. narbonense*) has 1-in (2.5-cm) azure-blue flowers with white centers on plants 18–24 in (45–60 cm) tall. Golden flax (*L. flavum*) grows 12–18 in (30–45 cm) tall with green leaves and bright yellow 1-in (2.5-cm) flowers.

■ **CULTIVATION AND CARE TIPS.** It grows best in full sun with sandy to average, moist but well-drained soil. Set plants 18 in (45 cm) apart. Protect the shallow roots with a mulch. Hardy to −20°F (−28°C).

■ **PROPAGATION.** Seed. Cuttings. Division in early spring.

■ **PESTS AND DISEASES.** Cutworms; rust.

LOBELIA

CARDINAL FLOWER, GREAT BLUE LOBELIA

WITH THE RIGHT GROWING conditions, both species can offer intensely colored spikes of asymmetrical flowers from summer to fall above low-growing clumps of leaves. They are effective when planted beside streams, in meadow gardens, lightly shaded beds or borders.

■ **SPECIES, VARIETIES, AND CULTIVARS.** Cardinal flower (*L. cardinalis*) has 1½-in (4-cm) scarlet red flowers on spikes 3–4 ft (90 cm–1.20 m) tall which attract hummingbirds. Hardy to −50°F (−46°C). Great blue lobelia (*L. siphilitica*) has 1-in (2.5-cm) dark blue flowers on 2–3-ft (60–90-cm) stems. Hardy to −20°F (−28°C). There are hybrid cultivars of both species.

■ **CULTIVATION AND CARE TIPS.** Both species grow best in light shade but tolerate full sun if the soil is always moist. A wet or moist, humus-rich soil is preferable. Staking may be needed. Although not always long-lived, they readily self-sow with the right growing conditions. Mulching keeps soil moist, improves hardiness, and encourages seedlings to grow. Set plants 12–18 in (30–45 cm) apart.

■ **PROPAGATION.** Seed. Remove and replant offsets in early fall.

■ **PESTS AND DISEASES.** Rust; crown rot; aphids; leafhoppers.

Lobelia cardinalis

Lupinus × 'RUSSELL HYBRIDS'

LUPINUS

LUPINE

LUPINES (*Lupinus* × 'Russell Hybrids') have showy 2–3-ft (60–90-cm) spikes of 1-in (2.5-cm) pea-like flowers in shades of white, yellow, pink, red, blue, or purple, either solid or bicolored, in early summer. The bushy plants have hand-shaped gray or bright green leaves. Lupines grow best in areas with cool, moist summers, and planted in the middle, center or back of flower beds and borders. They usually live about four years and do not readily transplant once established.

■ **CULTIVATION AND CARE TIPS.** They do well with either full sun or light shade and need humus-rich, moist but well-drained soil. Set plants 18–24 in (45–60 cm) apart. Deadhead regularly to promote second flowering. Mulch to conserve moisture and provide winter protection. Hardy to −20°F (−28°C).

■ **PROPAGATION.** Seed, which must be nicked with a file to germinate readily. Stem cuttings, with a portion of the root attached, in spring.

■ **PESTS AND DISEASES.** Blight; mildew; rust; aphids; plant bugs.

167

Lychnis chalcedonica

LYCHNIS

MALTESE CROSS, ROSE CAMPION, GERMAN CATCHFLY

THE VARIOUS species are useful in the front to middle of flower beds and borders or naturalized in meadow gardens. The flowers are good for cutting.

■ **SPECIES, VARIETIES, AND CULTIVARS.** The various species of lychnis suitable for the garden are very different in appearance. Maltese cross (*L. chalcedonica*) forms dense clumps with straight stems growing 2–3 ft (60–90 cm) tall with hairy, dark green leaves and clusters of 1-in (2.5-cm) orange-scarlet flowers from early to mid-summer. A second blooming occurs if faded flowers are removed. Plants are short-lived, but they readily reseed. Staking may be necessary.

Rose campion (*L. coronaria*) is a biennial with woolly, silvery-gray stems and leaves. Open and branching, the plants grow 18–24 in (45–60 cm) tall with 1-in (2.5-cm) magenta flowers, which attract butterflies. Plants readily reseed. Different forms are available.

Longer-lived German catchfly (*L. viscaria*) has hummocks of grassy, semi-evergreen foliage and slender 12–18-in (30–45-cm) stems that are sticky just beneath the bunches of ½-in (12-mm) flowers that bloom from late spring to midsummer. Different forms are available.

■ **CULTIVATION AND CARE TIPS.** The plants tolerate drought and grow best in full sun in average, very well-drained soil. Wet soil in winter is often fatal. Set plants 12 in (30 cm) apart. Hardy to −40°F (−40°C).

■ **PROPAGATION.** Seed. Division in spring or fall, usually every three or four years.

■ **PESTS AND DISEASES.** Leaf spot; root rot; rust; smut; whiteflies.

Lychnis coronaria

Lysimachia clethroides

LYSIMACHIA
GOOSENECK LOOSESTRIFE, YELLOW LOOSESTRIFE

GOOSENECK LOOSESTRIFE (*L. clethroides*) and yellow loosestrife (*L. punctata*) are very different in appearance, but share the common trait of being ideal for naturalizing beside streams or in other large, sunny or lightly shaded areas, as the roots tend to spread rapidly.

■ **SPECIES, VARIETIES, AND CULTIVARS.** Gooseneck loosestrife grows 2–3 ft (60–90 cm) tall. Good for cutting, the ½-in (12-mm) white flowers are in narrow spikes that curve gracefully to one side. Blooming continues for a long period during summer and foliage colors a bronze-yellow in the fall. Yellow loosestrife is the same height, but the 1-in (2.5-cm) yellow flowers are set in the axils where the leaves join the upright stems. Plants bloom from early to midsummer.

■ **CULTIVATION AND CARE TIPS.** Both types grow in average to humus-rich, moist soil. Drier soil is tolerated in light shade. Set plants 12 in (30 cm) apart from each other or 3 ft (90 cm) from other plants to allow the root to spread. Hardy to −30°F (−34°C).

■ **PROPAGATION.** Division in late fall or early spring. Seed.

■ **PESTS AND DISEASES.** Seldom bothered.

LYTHRUM
PURPLE LOOSESTRIFE

VARYING WIDELY IN HEIGHT and flower color, purple loosestrife is a very adaptable, low-maintenance, bushy plant that blooms from early summer until fall. Foliage is small and willow-like, providing fine texture in the garden, and the spikes of ¾-in (18-mm) flowers are produced abundantly.

■ **SPECIES, VARIETIES, AND CULTIVARS.** Purple loosestrife (*Lythrum salicaria*) has become widely naturalized by self-sowing. Many cultivars are available that have better color and are seemingly sterile and therefore not invasive. Most grow 3 ft (90 cm) tall.

■ **CULTIVATION AND CARE TIPS.** Although they naturally grow in wet meadows and beside streams, they also do well in moist, well-drained soil and even withstand dry conditions. Full sun is best, but light shade is tolerated. Set plants 18 in (45 cm) apart. Hardy to −40°F (−40°C).

■ **PROPAGATION.** Division in spring or fall. Root cuttings in early summer.

■ **PESTS AND DISEASES.** Seldom bothered.

Lythrum salicaria

169

Macleaya cordata

MACLEAYA

PLUME POPPY

BEST USED AS A specimen plant near a building or hedge, plume poppy (*Macleaya cordata*, also listed as *Bocconia cordata*) is bold and dramatic with its rounded, scalloped blue-green leaves with silvery undersides on 6–10-ft (1.80–3-m) stems. Fluffy, 12-in (30-cm) plumes of ½-in (12-mm) petal-less flowers bloom during summer, and the seed pods are attractive until frost. Both can be cut and dried for arrangements. Plants readily self-sow.

■ **CULTIVATION AND CARE TIPS.** It grows best in light shade in hotter regions, but full sun is tolerated in cooler areas. Plant in average moist to well-drained soil, spacing 3–4 ft (90 cm–1.20 m) apart. Hardy to −30°F (−34°C).

■ **PROPAGATION.** Division in spring. Seed.

■ **PESTS AND DISEASES.** Seldom bothered.

HOREHOUND

ALTHOUGH USUALLY CONSIDERED for the herb garden, silver horehound (*M. incanum*, also listed as *M. candidissimum*) is a good choice for flower beds and borders because it is one of the few silver-gray perennials that does not quickly rot in hot, humid climates. The wrinkled, woolly leaves are up to 2 in (5 cm) long on plants growing 2–3 ft (60–90 cm) tall and wide. The ⅛-in (3-mm) flowers are white and in rondels along the stems; remove unless self-sowing is desired, as the plant can become invasive.

■ **CULTIVATION AND CARE TIPS.** Drought-tolerant, it grows best in full sun with sandy, well-drained soil. Plants sprawl in rich, moist soil; control by shearing back when 12 in (30 cm) tall. Set plants 12 in (30 cm) apart. Hardy to −30°F (−34°C).

■ **PROPAGATION.** Seed. Division, if plants are not too woody.

■ **PESTS AND DISEASES.** Seldom bothered.

Marrubium incanum

Mertensia virginica

VIRGINIA BLUEBELLS

A BELOVED SPRING-BLOOMING wildflower, Virginia bluebells (*M. virginica*) are best grown in drifts under trees at the edge of a lawn. The foliage dies back in summer, so it is preferable to interplant with other plants. They grow 1–2 ft (30–60 cm) tall with oval, blue-green leaves and nodding clusters of 1-in (2.5-cm) fragrant, funnel-shaped flowers that are pinkish in bud, then becoming blue as they open. There are also pink- and white-flowered forms. Plants readily reseed.

■ **CULTIVATION AND CARE TIPS.** They grow best in light to full shade with acid, humus-rich, moist but well-drained soil that is drier when plants are dormant. Set plants 8–12 in (20–30 cm) apart, with the crown 1 in (2.5 cm) deep. Hardy to −30°F (−34°C).

■ **PROPAGATION.** Seed sown as soon as ripe. Division in fall.

■ **PESTS AND DISEASES.** Slugs.

Monarda didyma 'CAMBRIDGE SCARLET'

MONARDA

BEE BALM, WILD BERGAMOT

L ONG-LIVED, EASILY GROWN, and adaptable, bee balm (*M. didyma*) blooms for much of the summer with unusually shaped flowers in shades of white, pink, lavender, magenta, red or burgundy. Excellent for cutting, the 2–3-in (5–7.5-cm) flowers attract hummingbirds and bees. The dark green leaves have a minty scent, and both flowers and leaves can be dried for adding to potpourris. It is a superb choice for the middle to back of borders or center of beds as well as for naturalizing as they spread by runners. Growing to 2–3 ft (60–90 cm) tall with slightly hairy foliage, a number of named cultivars are available. Wild bergamot (*M. fistulosa*) grows 3–4 ft (90 cm–1.20 m) tall with softly hairy leaves and lavender to purple 1½-in (4-cm) flowers. It can be invasive, so is best grown in naturalized areas.

■ **CULTIVATION AND CARE TIPS.** Both bee balm and wild bergamot readily grow in both full sun and light shade, with more soil moisture necessary in full sun. A wide range of soils are tolerated, but the best is a humus-rich, moist but well-drained one. Wild bergamot, however, is more tolerant of poorer, drier soil and hotter summers. Deadhead regularly to encourage additional flowering through the summer. Cut plants back to the ground in the fall. Set plants 18 in (45 cm) apart. Hardy to −30°F (−34°C).

■ **PROPAGATION.** Division in spring every three or four years. Seed for the species.

■ **PESTS AND DISEASES.** Leaf spot; mildew; rust; stem borers.

NEPETA

CATMINT

RELATED TO CATNIP, two very similar types of cat-mint are lovely in the garden because their delicate texture and color blend so readily with other flowers and plants. The sprawling mounds are useful as an edging, in a rock garden, in raised beds or walls, or at the front of beds and borders. Small, heart-shaped, hairy gray leaves densely cover the 12–18-in (30–45-cm) plants. Spikes of ¼-in (6-mm) softly colored blue or white flowers in spring and early summer may rebloom if plants are cut back by half after the first blooming.

■ **SPECIES, VARIETIES, AND CULTIVARS.** *N. × faassenii* is sterile and does not self-sow so plants must be propagated by division. *N. mussinii* can be raised from seed. 'Blue Wonder' is a recommended cultivar.

■ **CULTIVATION AND CARE TIPS.** They grow best in full sun in sandy, well-drained soil. Plants have more compact, attractive growth in poor soil and are tolerant of drought and hot summers. Set plants 12–18 in (30–45 cm) apart. Hardy to −40°F (−40°C).

■ **PROPAGATION.** Both types may be divided in spring. Seed for *N. mussinii*.

■ **PESTS AND DISEASES.** Rust; leafhoppers.

Nepeta x faassenii

Oenothera tetragona

OENOTHERA

SUNDROP, MISSOURI PRIMROSE

BEAUTIFUL PINK OR YELLOW fragrant flowers, bloom-ing for much of the summer, have made these peren-nials popular for rock gardens, as an edging, or at the front of beds and borders.

■ **SPECIES, VARIETIES, AND CULTIVARS.** What are purchased as sundrops may be *O. fruticosa* var. *youngii* or *O. tetragona* as they are similar. They grow 18–24 in (45–60 cm) tall with narrow, shiny green leaves and 1-in (2.5-cm) saucer-shaped, yellow flowers blooming during the day. The Missouri primrose or Ozark sundrop (*O. missourensis*) has trailing stems 12 in (30 cm) long and yellow flowers 4 in (10 cm) across, which open in the evening and remain so until the following evening. The seed pods can be dried for bouquets. The showy primrose (*O. speciosa*) grows 18 in (45 cm) tall with 2-in (5-cm) pink or white flowers. It can become invasive so choose the site carefully.

■ **CULTIVATION AND CARE TIPS.** Both are easily grown in full sun with average well-drained soil. They are tolerant of poor, dry conditions and heat. Set plants 18 in (45 cm) apart. Hardy to −20°F (−28°C).

■ **PROPAGATION.** Seed. Division in spring every three or four years.

■ **PESTS AND DISEASES.** Aphids; leaf spot; rust.

ORNAMENTAL GRASSES

ORNAMENTAL GRASSES offer the gardener wonderfully fine textures in a wide range of sizes, shapes and colors. They often also provide year-round interest because of the long-lasting seed-heads foliage that persists during the winter. They can be used in many different ways, in flower beds and borders, as specimens against walls, or among shrubs, massed in drifts, used as ground cover, or as part of a meadow garden. Many of the grass flowers are excellent for using fresh or dried in arrangements.

■ **SPECIES, VARIETIES, AND CULTIVARS.** Very supple and graceful, feather reed grass (*Calamagrostis* × *acutiflora* 'Stricta') has very thin pale green leaves 30 in (75 cm) tall and narrow flowers growing 5 ft (1.50 m) tall. These open pale gold in midsummer, turn brown by fall, and persist in winter, shading to gray. Wild oats (*Chasmanthium latifolium*, also listed as *Uniola latifolia*) has broad, dark green leaves 2 ft (60 cm) tall and spread slowly to 3 ft (90 cm) across. Fall-blooming, the golden-tan flowers are flattened spikes on wiry, arching stems. Light shade is tolerated. Blue wild rye (*Elymus glaucus*) has flat leaves growing 4 ft (1.20 m) tall with late-summer flowers. It spreads readily and is good as a ground cover. Divide every two to three years. Hardy to −50°F (−46°C). Blue fescue (*Festuca cinerea*, also listed as *F. ovina* 'Glauca') is a very fine-textured, spiky grass forming rounded clumps 8–10 in (20–25 cm) tall. Plants bloom in June, but these are best clipped off. Blue oat grass (*Helictotrichon sempervirens*) forms stiff, spiky clumps of fine-textured blue-green leaves 2 ft (60 cm) tall. Flower stems grow 4 ft (1.20 m) tall but are not particularly showy. Japanese

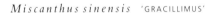

Miscanthus sinensis 'GRACILLIMUS'

Pennisetum alopecuroides

blood grass (*Imperata cylindrica* 'Red Baron') has broad, flat, spiky, 2-ft (60-cm) leaves of a striking deep red. It is useful among gray-leaved plants and in rock gardens. Hardy to −20°F (−28°C). There are a number of cultivars of eulalia grass (*Miscanthus sinensis*), with most having 5–7-ft (1.50–2.1-m) silken, feathery plumes in late summer that persist well through the winter. Most also have graceful, arching foliage growing 4–6 ft (1.20–1.80 m) tall. Fountain grass (*Pennisetum alopecuroides*) has typical grassy foliage growing 30 in (75 cm) tall with an abundance of fuzzy, bottle-brush, 5-in (12.5-cm) flowers that are green in midsummer, changing to brown in fall, and tan in winter. Ribbon grass (*Phalaris arundinacea* 'Picta') is a vigorous, spreading plant with green-and-white striped leaves growing 2–3 ft (60–90 cm) tall. Hardy to −40°F (−40°C).

■ **CULTIVATION AND CARE TIPS.** Of the dozens of ornamental grasses, the ones listed are most readily available and easiest to grow. They have similar requirements, including full sun and a humus-rich, moist but well-drained soil. Average to poor soil and dry conditions are usually tolerated. Trim plants back to ground level before growth begins in the spring. It may take several years for ornamental grasses to become fully established. Hardy to −30°F (−34°C) unless otherwise noted.

Paeonia 'ANGELUS'

PAEONIA

PEONY

P EONIES ARE AMONG the most widely grown of perennials and will live for decades. Blooming in late spring and early summer, the bushy plants grow 2–3 ft (60–90 cm) tall with lush, shiny foliage. Use peonies in flower beds and borders, in front of shrubs, as a low hedge or beside a wall.

■ **SPECIES, VARIETIES, AND CULTIVARS.** There are thousands of hybrid cultivars of the common, or Chinese, peony (*P. lactiflora*). The 3–6-in (7.5–15-cm) wide blooms may be shades of white, creamy yellow, pink, or red and in one of five forms: single, with eight petals and a prominent cluster of yellow stamens; Japanese, with a carnation-like center and a saucer-shaped petal collar; anemone, similar to Japanese but shaggier; semidouble, with stamens apparent; and double, with stamens missing or hidden. Excellent for cutting, the flowers of some varieties are fragrant. By choosing early, midseason, and late-blooming kinds, the blooming period can be extended for six weeks. *P. officinalis*, also called common peony, or Memorial Day peony, is similar to the Chinese peony with 4-in (10-cm) single crimson flowers with yellow stamens.

■ **CULTIVATION AND CARE TIPS.** All peonies are easily grown in humus-rich, moist but well-drained soil in full sun, or light shade in hotter areas. Set the eyes, or red sprouts, 1 in (2.5 cm) deep and 2–3 ft (60–90 cm) apart in fall before the ground freezes. Taller types may need staking. To prevent botrytis blight, cut off all stems and leaves in fall. Hardy to −40°F (−40°C), a mulch is beneficial in areas −20°F (−28°C) or colder with no snow cover. Winter chilling is necessary, and peonies do not grow and bloom well in subtropical areas.

■ **PROPAGATION.** Although best left undisturbed, peonies can be divided in fall, cutting roots apart with a knife, with each piece having three eyes.

■ **PESTS AND DISEASES.** Botrytis blight; snails; slugs.

Paeonia 'MONS. JULES ELIE'

Papaver orientale

PAPAVER

ORIENTAL POPPY

AN OLD-FASHIONED FAVORITE, Oriental poppies (*P. orientale*) are beloved for the early summer blooming, papery translucent orange, red, pink, salmon, or white flowers, often with a purple-black blotch in the center. The silver-green, rough-textured, fern-like leaves and the 6-in (15-cm) flowers grow on plants 2–4 ft (60 cm–1.20 m) tall. The flowers are good for cutting if picked just as buds begin to open in early morning and the stem ends are seared in a flame. Plants go dormant after flowering, so they are best planted in beds or borders near other perennials. They are long-lived and best left undisturbed for at least five years.

■ **CULTIVATION AND CARE TIPS.** They are easily grown in full sun with average well-drained soil. Poor drainage in winter is usually fatal. Staking may be necessary with taller types. Set plants 18 in (45 cm) apart, with the crown 3 in (7.5 cm) deep. Hardy to −30°F (−34°C). Both a summer and winter mulch is beneficial.

■ **PROPAGATION.** Division in late summer or fall when new growth appears. Root cuttings in late summer.

■ **PESTS AND DISEASES.** Blight; aphids.

  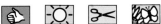

PHLOX

PHLOX

PHLOXES ARE A LARGE, diverse group of perennials that provide a wide range of sizes, shapes and colors. As such, they are indispensable in a garden. They are easily grown and bloom for long periods, with each type having the distinctive five-petaled, flat-faced flower. The taller types are best used in beds and borders; the shorter, creeping types in wildflower and woodland gardens; and the mat-forming ones spilling over the edges of raised beds, in walls or rock gardens.

■ **SPECIES, VARIETIES, AND CULTIVARS.** Carolina phlox (*P. caroliniana*, also listed as *P. suffruticosa*) grows in clumps 3 ft (90 cm) tall with loose, somewhat flat clusters of ¾-in (18-mm) purple to pink flowers in early summer. Resistant to mildew and spider mite, it is also tolerant of light shade.

Wild sweet william (*P. divaricata*) grows 12 in (30 cm) tall with rapidly spreading creeping stems. The 1-in (2.5-cm) light blue, lavender, or white flowers bloom in loose, flat clusters in early spring. It grows best in light shade.

Meadow phlox (*P. maculata*, but usually listed as *P. caroliniana*, which it resembles) grows in clumps with strong 2–4-ft (60-cm–1.20-m) stems and large clusters of fragrant, ½-in (12-mm) purple, pink, or white flowers. Restistant to mildew and seldom requiring staking, cutting back encourages a second bloom.

Phlox divaricata 'CHATTAHOOCHEE'

Phlox paniculata

Garden phlox (*P. paniculata*) grows in clumps 3–4 ft (90 cm–1.20 m) tall and blooms from summer to early fall with large, open clusters of 1-in (2.5-cm) flowers in shades of pink, white, red, or pale blue. They are temperamental plants, susceptible to mildew, and do best in cool-summer areas.

Creeping phlox (*P. stolonifera*) grows 12 in (30 cm) tall with creeping stems. The spring-blooming ¾-in (18-mm) flowers may be purple, violet, or blue.

Ground, or moss, pink (*P. subulata*) is a mat-forming plant growing 6 in (15 cm) high with needle-like leaves. It is densely covered with bright purple, pink, or white, ¾-in (18-mm) flowers in early spring.

■ **CULTIVATION AND CARE TIPS.** They grow best in humus-rich, moist but well-drained soil. Set plants 12–24 in (30–60 cm) apart. Hardy to −40°F (−40°C).

■ **PROPAGATION.** Division in spring, usually every three or four years. Cuttings.

■ **PESTS AND DISEASES.** Mildew; leaf spot; beetles; spider mites; plant bugs.

OBEDIENT PLANT, FALSE DRAGONHEAD

EASY TO GROW, obedient plant (*P. virginiana*, also listed as *Dracocephalum virginianum*) grows in bushy clumps 2–4 ft (60 cm–1.20 m) tall with stiff, wand-like spikes of pink, magenta, rose, lilac, or white tubular 1-in (2.5-cm) flowers. Blooming for a long time in summer and fall, the flowers are excellent for cutting. It spreads rapidly and is useful in wildflower gardens and beside streams. The named cultivars are better for more formal areas of the garden, such as traditional beds and borders.

■ **CULTIVATION AND CARE TIPS.** It grows best in full sun with average, moist, slightly acid soil. Drier soil is tolerated, especially in light shade, but plants will be shorter. Set plants 18–24 in (45–60 cm) apart. Hardy to −40°F (−40°C).

■ **PROPAGATION.** Division in spring every other year.

■ **PESTS AND DISEASES.** Rust; mildew; aphids.

Physostegia virginiana

Polygonatum odoratum thunbergii 'VARIEGATUM'

PLATYCODON

BALLOON FLOWER

FORMING 18–30-in (45–75-cm) tall, stiffly bushy plants, balloon flower (*P. grandiflorus*) derives its common name from the shape of the bud, which opens into a 2-in (5-cm), cup-like, star-shaped blue flower. This long-blooming perennial also has many other varieties. Flowers are beautiful in arrangements; stem ends must be seared in a flame.

■ **CULTIVATION AND CARE TIPS.** This easily grown, adaptable plant does not start to sprout until late in the spring, so the location must be marked well. Blue- and white-flowered cultivars thrive in full sun, but pink flowers fade unless in light shade. Provide average to sandy, well-drained soil; poor drainage in winter is fatal. The plants may take several years to become established, and if moved, must be dug deeply to get all of the long roots, which spread slowly. Division is seldom necessary and the plants are long-lived. Plants also self-sow, but not rampantly. Staking is necessary with taller cultivars. Deadhead regularly to prolong blooming. Set plants 12–18 in (30–45 cm) apart, with the crown just below the soil surface; a group of three plants in the middle of a bed or border is most effective. Although hardy to −40°F (−40°C), some loose winter protection is often necessary for plants to survive.

■ **PROPAGATION.** Cut off outer sections of crown in spring when shoots are 1 in (2.5 cm) tall. Seed.

■ **PESTS AND DISEASES.** Root rot; Japanese beetles

Platycodon grandiflorus

POLYGONATUM

SOLOMON'S SEAL

THE DIFFERENT FORMS OF Solomon's seal are all similar in appearance, with arching, unbranched stems of pointed, oval leaves and drooping, tubular, white or cream flowers in late spring and early summer.

■ **SPECIES, VARIETIES, AND CULTIVARS.** Mainly grown as handsome foliage plants for light to full shade, *P. biflorum* grows 1–3 ft (30–90 cm) tall, *P. commutatum* (also listed as *P. canaliculatum*) 4–6 ft (1.20–1.80 m) tall, and *P.* × *hybridum* (also listed as *P. multiflorum*) 3 ft (90 cm) tall. The variegated Japanese Solomon's seal (*P. odoratum thunbergii* 'Variegatum') growing 2–3 ft (60–90 cm) tall with leaves edged in creamy white, is considered the most beautiful form.

■ **CULTIVATION AND CARE TIPS.** The rhizomatous roots spread slowly forming handsome colonies. Long-lived, it is seldom invasive and division is rarely needed. It thrives in humus-rich, moist but well-drained soil; dry soil is however tolerated. Set plants 18–24 in (45–60 cm) apart. Hardy to −30°F (−34°C).

■ **PROPAGATION.** Division in spring or fall. Seed.

■ **PESTS AND DISEASES.** Seldom bothered.

PRIMULA

PRIMROSE

HUNDREDS OF SPECIES and thousands of cultivars of primrose have captured the hearts of gardeners for the bright colors they bring to a lightly shaded spring garden. Most types form a ground-hugging clump with long, narrow or rounded, oval leaves and leafless stalks bearing clusters of five-petaled, semidouble, or double flowers. Although generally short-lived, primroses are readily started from seed.

■ **SPECIES, VARIETIES, AND CULTIVARS.** The alpine primrose (*P. auricula*) grows 8 in (20 cm) tall with clusters of fragrant, spring-blooming, 1-in (2.5-cm) flowers in a wide range of muted colours with a white eye. Hybrid forms are more easily grown than the species. Hardy to −40°F (−40°C). The Himalayan primrose (*P. denticulata*) has rounded, 2-in (5-cm) heads of lilac flowers in spring on 10-in (25-cm) stems. Hardy to −30°F (−34°C). The Japanese primrose (*P. japonica*) has whorls of 1-in (2.5-cm) magenta, crimson, pink, or white flowers spaced at intervals along stalks growing 2 ft (60 cm) tall. It readily self-seeds, especially if grown in constantly moist soil, such as on banks of streams. Hardy to −20°F (−28°C). Most widely grown of all primroses is the polyanthus primrose (*P. × polyantha*), which grows 10 in (25 cm) tall with single or

Primula x polyantha

Primula denticulata

double, 1–2-in (2.5–5-cm) flowers in almost every conceivable color. Generally hardy to −30°F (−34°C), but this depends on the cultivar. Siebold primrose (*P. sieboldii*) has crinkly, scalloped leaves with clusters of pink, rose, or white 1–2-in (2.5–5-cm) flowers in late spring and early summer on 12-in (30-cm) plants. It is somewhat tolerant of hot conditions. Hardy to −20°F (−28°C). English, or common, primrose (*P. vulgaris*, also listed as *P. acaulis*) has lightly fragrant, 1-in (2.5-cm), yellow flowers in early spring on 6-in (15-cm) plants with evergreen leaves. There are a number of cultivars and strains in a wide range of other colors. Hardy to −20°F (−28°C).

■ **CULTIVATION AND CARE TIPS.** Most types grow best with high, light shade and humus-rich, moist but well-drained soil. A summer mulch and watering during dry periods is necessary. A loose winter mulch is beneficial in cold areas with minimal snow cover. Set plants 12 in (30 cm) apart.

■ **PROPAGATION.** Division after flowering. Seed.

■ **PESTS AND DISEASES.** Spider mites; slugs; leaf spot; rot.

Pulmonaria saccharata 'MISS MOON'

PULMONARIA
BLUE LUNGWORT, BETHLEHEM SAGE

SMALL, CREEPING PLANTS with hairy, dark green or mottled leaves and spring-blooming pink, blue or white flowers, the subtlety of pulmonarias is best appreciated when they are grown at the front of a shady border, as an edging to a path, or planted in drifts among shrubs and trees. The foliage is attractive throughout the growing season.

■ **SPECIES, VARIETIES, AND CULTIVARS.** Blue lungwort (*P. angustifolia*) grows 6–12 inches (15–30 cm) tall with narrow, dark green leaves. Dense clusters of pink buds open to ½-in (12-mm) blue flowers. Bethlehem sage (*P. saccharata*) grows 12–18 in (30–45 cm) tall with semi-evergreen leaves mottled with gray or white spots. The clusters of ½-in (12-mm) flowers may be white, blue, or pink.

■ **CULTIVATION AND CARE TIPS.** They grow best in light shade with a humus-rich, moist but well-drained soil. Set plants 12 in (30 cm) apart. Division is seldom necessary unless plants become overcrowded, and plants are not invasive. Hardy to −30°F (−34°C).

■ **PROPAGATION.** Division in fall.

■ **PESTS AND DISEASES.** Slugs.

CONEFLOWER, BLACK-EYED SUSAN

THE BOLD, BRIGHT golden-yellow, daisy-like flowers blooming from midsummer to fall have made the various coneflowers popular for generations of gardeners. Some are annuals, biennials, or short-lived perennials, but two are long-lived, low maintenance perennials useful from the front to the middle of beds and borders, massed in large drifts, or planted in meadow gardens. Flowers are good for cutting, and the dark cones remaining after the flowers have faded are eye-catching in the winter garden.

■ **SPECIES, VARIETIES, AND CULTIVARS.** Orange coneflower, or black-eyed Susan (*R. fulgida*), forms 2–3-ft (60–90-cm) tall bushy, branching plants with hairy leaves and 3–4-in (7.5–10-cm) flowers with yellow-orange petals surrounding a brown-black cone. The widely sold cultivar *R. fulgida* var. *sullivantii* 'Goldsturm' grows 2 ft tall and produces masses of large flowers. *R. nitida* grows 3–4 ft (90 cm–1.20 m) tall with lemon-yellow flowers with greenish centers.

■ **CULTIVATION AND CARE TIPS.** They readily grow in full sun and average to moist, well-drained soil. Set 18 in (45 cm) apart. Hardy to −40°F (−40°C).

■ **PROPAGATION.** Division in early spring every three or four years. Seed.

■ **PESTS AND DISEASES.** Leaf miners; mildew; aphids; rust.

Rudbeckia fulgida

SALVIA

SAGE

THE GENUS *Salvia* is a very large one, with annual, biennial and perennial forms, including the popular annual scarlet sage as well as the culinary herb sage. The longest-lived perennial sage, easiest to grow and best for low-maintenance gardens, is violet sage (*S.* × *superba*, also listed as *S. nemorosa*), which has an abundance of 6–12-in (15–30-cm) stalks of dark purple, ½-in (12-mm) flowers. These are good for fresh or dried arrangements. Plants grow 18–36 in (45–90 cm) tall with gray-green leaves.

■ **CULTIVATION AND CARE TIPS.** It does best with full sun and average, well-drained soil, and is tolerant of drought. Poorly drained soil in winter is usually fatal. Set plants 12–18 in (30–45 cm) apart. Deadhead regularly to prolong blooming. Although hardy to −20°F (−28°C), a loose winter mulch is beneficial.

■ **PROPAGATION.** Division in spring or fall.

■ **PESTS AND DISEASES.** Whiteflies; leaf spot; rust; scale.

Salvia x superba 'MAY NIGHT'

Scabiosa caucasica

SCABIOSA

PINCUSHION FLOWER

ABOVE CLUMPS OF finely cut, gray-green foliage, pincushion flower (*S. caucasica*) sends up stalks of blue, lavender-blue, or white, 2–3-in (5–7.5-cm), richly textured flowers throughout the summer that are excellent for cutting. It grows 12–18 in (30–45 cm) tall, and is best enjoyed when planted in groups of three near the front of beds and borders. The best cultivar is 'Fama', with intense blue flowers on sturdy stems 18–24 in (45–60 cm) tall.

■ **CULTIVATION AND CARE TIPS.** It is easily grown in full sun with sandy to average, neutral to alkaline, well-drained soil. It does not do well under very hot conditions, unless grown in light shade. Set plants 12 in (30 cm) apart. Hardy to −40°F (−40°C). Deadhead regularly to prolong blooming.

■ **PROPAGATION.** Division in spring, if necessary. Fresh seed sown in fall.

■ **PESTS AND DISEASES.** Slugs.

Sedum 'AUTUMN JOY'

SEDUM

STONECROP

AN ENORMOUS GROUP of plants with hundreds of species, varieties, and cultivars, stonecrops are noted for their handsome succulent foliage, their showy, butterfly-attracting, long-lasting clusters of ¼-in (6-mm) flowers, and, particularly, their drought tolerance. Many are creeping plants especially good for rock gardens, draping over walls and steps, or edging paths. Taller types, growing to 2 ft (60 cm), are handsome additions to the middle of beds and borders.

■ **SPECIES, VARIETIES, AND CULTIVARS.** The most widely grown stonecrop is the hybrid 'Autumn Joy' (also called 'Indian Chief'). Growing 2 ft (60 cm) tall with gray-green leaves, flowering starts in early fall with the clusters of tiny flowers opening pale pink; gradually they deepen to salmon rose-red, then coppery bronze by late fall and winter. These can be used in dried bouquets or left on for landscape interest in the winter. It is tolerant of moist soil and light shade, but does best in full sun with well-drained soil.

Its parent is the showy stonecrop (*S. spectabile*), which grows 2 ft (60 cm) tall with pink flowers. October daphne (*S. sieboldii*) is a trailing 6-in (15-cm) plant with semi-evergreen gray leaves and pink flowers in late fall.

The purple-leaved great stonecrop (*S. maximum* 'Atropurpureum') sprawls stiffly with 2-ft (60-cm) stems; it has red-purple foliage and dusty pink flowers in early fall. Aizoon stonecrop (*S. aizoon*) grows 12–18 in (30–45 cm) tall with bright green leaves on erect stems and yellow flowers in summer. *S. kamtschaticum* grows 6–12 in (15–30 cm) tall with upright stems and yellow-orange flowers from midsummer until fall.

■ **CULTIVATION AND CARE TIPS.** Tough, adaptable and easily grown, they tolerate a wide range of conditions, but do best in full sun and any well-drained soil. Set shorter types 12 in (30 cm) apart and taller ones 18–24 in (45–60 cm) apart. Hardy to −30°F (−34°C).

■ **PROPAGATION.** Division in spring. Cuttings in summer.

■ **PESTS AND DISEASES.** Seldom bothered.

Sedum kamtschaticum

Smilacina racemosa

SMILACINA
FALSE SOLOMON'S SEAL

FALSE SOLOMON'S SEAL (*S. racemosa*) has 18–36-in (45–60-cm) arching stems of pointed oval leaves resembling Solomon's seal. The flowers, produced in late spring, are 4–6-in (10–15-cm) feathery clusters of tiny creamy-white blooms, that, in late summer, become clusters of bright red berries. False Solomon's seal is a good foliage plant for naturalizing in light to full shade, spreading by thick rhizomatous roots, and is especially effective interplanted with spring-blooming bulbs or ferns, or planted either behind hostas or in front of shade-loving shrubs.

■ **CULTIVATION AND CARE TIPS.** It grows best in slightly acid, humus-rich, moist but well-drained soil. Space 12–18 in (30–45 cm) apart. Hardy to −30°F (−34°C).

■ **PROPAGATION.** Division in spring, which is seldom necessary except for increase. Seed sown in fall.

■ **PESTS AND DISEASES.** Seldom bothered.

SOLIDAGO
GOLDENROD

FORMING BROAD, UPRIGHT clumps 18–42 in (45 cm–1.05 m) tall with branching, graceful golden-yellow flowers, goldenrod blooms from midsummer into fall. The flowers are good for fresh arrangements as well as dried or preserved in glycerin for winter bouquets. Plant in the middle of beds and borders, mass in drifts, or naturalize in meadow gardens. They can be really stunning if planted in groups of three. Given rich soil, the roots spread rapidly, and some types self-sow. In the wild, there are a number of species of goldenrod, which readily hybridize, so specific identification is complicated and plants started from seed are variable. Buying named cultivars from nurseries is the best way to get better-flowering forms.

■ **CULTIVATION AND CARE TIPS.** It is very easily grown in full sun and almost any well-drained soil ranging from sandy to average. Light shade is tolerated. Set plants 18 in (45 cm) apart. Hardy to −30°F (−34°C).

■ **PROPAGATION.** Division in spring every three years.

■ **PESTS AND DISEASES.** Rust.

Solidago

■ **CULTIVATION AND CARE TIPS.** Both forms grow well in poor to average, well-drained soils. Plant big betony in full sun to light shade and lamb's ears in full sun. Set plants 12 in (30 cm) apart. Hardy to −30°F (−34°C).

■ **PROPAGATION.** Division in spring or fall, every fourth year or when plants die out in the center. Seed.

■ **PESTS AND DISEASES.** Seldom bothered, except lamb's ears may rot in hot, humid climates.

Stachys byzantina

Stachys macrantha

STACHYS

BIG BETONY, LAMB'S EARS

THE TWO FORMS OF stachys useful in the garden are very dissimilar. Big betony (*S. macrantha*, also listed as *S. grandiflora*) has hairy, dark green, heart-shaped leaves that are wrinkled with scalloped edges. In late spring and early summer, whorled spikes of 1½-in (4-cm) violet, lavender-pink, or rosy pink flowers reach 18–24 in (45–60 cm) tall. Plant in at the front of beds and borders and use the flowers for cutting. Lamb's ears (*S. byzantina*, also listed as *S. olympica* or *S. lanata*) form 2-ft (60-cm) ground-hugging mats of 4–6-in (10–15-cm) long white, thick, softly furry leaves with 12–18-in (30–45-cm) spikes of ½-in (12-mm) magenta flowers. The flowers are produced intermittently all summer; some gardeners prefer to cut them off to improve appearance and prevent self-sowing. This long-lived species makes a dense ground cover accent for the front of beds and borders, in a rock garden, or as an edging.

Stokesia laevis

STOKESIA

STOKES' ASTER

STOKES' ASTER (*S. laevis*) forms stiff, branching plants with long, narrow leaves that are evergreen in warmer climates. Flowers are lacy, fringed, blue or white, and 4 in (10 cm) across on 12–24-in (30–60-cm) stems. Excellent for cutting, it is at its best planted in groups of three at the front of the border.

■ **CULTIVATION AND CARE TIPS.** Long-lived, it grows well in full sun with average, well-drained soil. Poor drainage in winter is usually fatal. Set plants 12–18 in (30–45 cm) apart. Deadhead regularly to prolong blooming. Hardy to −20°F (−28°C), with a loose winter mulch beneficial in colder areas to prevent roots heaving out of the ground.

■ **PROPAGATION.** Division in spring every four years. Seed.

■ **PESTS AND DISEASES.** Seldom bothered.

THALICTRUM

MEADOWRUE

AIRY CLOUDS OF LAVENDER, yellow, or pink flowers above delicate blue-green leaves give meadowrues an elegant, fine-textured appearance that enhances the back of beds and borders, banks of streams or wildflower gardens. The flowers are good for cutting.

■ **SPECIES, VARIETIES, AND CULTIVARS.** Columbine meadowrue (*T. aquilegifolium*) grows 3 ft (90 cm) tall with columbine-like leaves. Branching, crowded clusters of powderpuff-like, ½-in (12-mm) lavender flowers bloom in late spring. Lavender mist meadowrue (*T. rochebrunianum*) grows 3–5 ft (90 cm–1.50 m) tall with leaves resembling maidenhair fern. The loose, open flower clusters, blooming in summer, are composed of ½-in (12-mm), five-petaled, purple or pink-lavender blooms centered with bright yellow stamens. Dusty meadowrue (*T. flavum*, also listed as *T. speciosissimum*) grows 3–5 ft (90 cm–1.50 m) tall with masses of fluffy yellow flowers in summer.

■ **CULTIVATION AND CARE TIPS.** In cool-summer climates, they grow well in full sun but in hotter areas, light shade and a summer mulch is preferred. Provide humus-rich, moist but well-drained soil. Staking is necessary for lavender mist and dusty meadowrues. Set plants 18–24 in (45–60 cm) apart, preferably in groups of three. Plants take several years to become established. Hardy to −20°F (−28°C).

■ **PROPAGATION.** Division every four or five years in spring. Fresh seed sown in the fall.

■ **PESTS AND DISEASES.** Mildew; rust; aphids.

Thalictrum flavum

Thermopsis villosa

THERMOPSIS

CAROLINA THERMOPSIS

RESEMBLING LUPINE, carolina thermopsis (*T. villosa*, also listed as *T. caroliniana*) has 8–12-in (20–30-cm) long spikes of ½-in (12-mm) yellow, pea-like flowers on stout stalks 3–5 ft (90 cm–1.50 m) tall in early to midsummer. Plants slowly spread to form clumps 3 ft (90 cm) across. Long-lived, even surviving neglect, it has foliage attractive all summer long and deep, drought-resistant roots. Use at the back of borders or the center of beds as well as in a meadow garden. The flowers are long-lasting in arrangements if cut when only the bottom flowers are open.

■ **CULTIVATION AND CARE TIPS.** It grows easily in poor to average, well-drained soil in full sun, although light shade is tolerated. Staking may be necessary with older plants or in windy sites. Set plants 2–3 ft (60–90 cm) apart. Hardy to −40°F (−40°C).

■ **PROPAGATION.** Division is seldom necessary and difficult because of the deep roots. Cuttings in late spring. Fresh seed sown in late summer.

■ **PESTS AND DISEASES.** Seldom bothered.

SPIDERWORT

LONG AND NARROW, the graceful, grasslike leaves of spiderwort (*T. × andersoniana*, also listed as *T. virginiana*) form robust clumps 2–3 ft (60–75 cm) tall. At intervals along the stems, clusters of three-petaled flowers, 1 in (2.5 cm) or more across, bloom throughout summer, with each flower lasting a day. A number of cultivars provide colors in shades of blue, pink, mauve, maroon, rose-purple, or white. Use spiderworts in beds and borders or naturalistic woodland gardens.

■ **CULTIVATION AND CARE TIPS.** Durable, long-lived plants, tolerating a wide range of conditions, it easily grows in full sun to light shade and poor to average, well-drained soil. Trimming stems to the ground in midsummer encourages new growth and fall flowering. Set plants 18 in (45 cm) apart. Hardy to −30°F (−34°C).

■ **PROPAGATION.** Division in spring or fall, as needed to control.

■ **PESTS AND DISEASES.** Seldom bothered.

Tradescantia x andersoniana

Veronica latifolia 'CRATER LAKE BLUE'

VERONICA

SPEEDWELL, VERONICA

THE GROWTH HABIT of speedwells ranges from low, creeping forms to upright, bushy types, but all have pointed spikes of flowers in shades of blue as well as purple, pink, red, or white that are excellent for cutting. Many kinds are low-maintenance perennials with a long blooming period, suitable either for the front or middle of beds and borders.

■ **SPECIES, VARIETIES, AND CULTIVARS.** One of the best is 'Crater Lake Blue', a cultivar of Hungarian speedwell (*V. latifolia*, also listed as *V. teucrium*). Somewhat sprawling, it has ½-in (12-mm) navy blue flowers in late spring and early summer on plants 12 in (30 cm) tall with narrow, dark green, toothed leaves. Lowgrowing, woolly speedwell (*V. incana*) has silver-gray leaves on 6-in (15-cm) clumps and 12–18-in (30–45-cm) stems of ¼-in (6-mm) lilac-blue flowers in summer.

The best form of the beach, or clump, speedwell is

V. longifolia var. *subsessilis*. It forms clumps of strong 2-ft (60-cm) stems with toothed, pointed leaves and densely packed spires of ½-in (12-mm) royal blue flowers bloom from midsummer to fall. Spike speedwell (*V. spicata*) grows 12–18 in (30–45 cm) tall with spikes of bright blue, ¼-in (6-mm) flowers during summer.

■ **CULTIVATION AND CARE TIPS.** Long-lived, they grow best in full sun, but tolerate light shade. Provide average, well-drained soil. Poorly drained soil in winter is often fatal. Remove faded flower spikes to prolong blooming. Set plants 12–18 in (30–45 cm) apart, singly or in groups of three. Hardy to −30°F (−34°C).

■ **PROPAGATION.** Division in spring or fall every four years.

■ **PESTS AND DISEASES.** Seldom bothered.

VIOLA

VIOLET, PANSY, JOHNNY-JUMP-UP

DIMINUTIVE VIOLETS AND pansies have been grown and loved for centuries. Of the hundreds of species and many cultivars, some are weeds and others rare plants for the collector's garden. A few species can be singled out for use in front of beds and borders, in wildflower gardens, as a ground cover, or as an edging along paths. The flowers can be used in tiny bouquets.

■ **SPECIES, VARIETIES, AND CULTIVARS.** Horned, or tufted, violet (*V. cornuta*) forms neat plants 6–8 in (15–20 cm) tall with 1-in (2.5-cm) violet, maroon, apricot, purple, yellow, or white flowers produced all summer long in full sun in areas where summers are cool and moist. With a summer mulch and light shade plants grow and bloom well in hotter areas. Hardy to −10°F (−23°C). Marsh blue violet (*V. cucullata*) grows 1 ft (30 cm) tall and slowly forms large patches from the spreading rhizomatous roots. It blooms in late spring and early summer with ½-in (12-mm) flowers of differ-

ent colors depending on the cultivar. Hardy to −30°F (−34°C). Sweet violet (*V. odorata*) blooms in spring on 8-in (20-cm) plants that spread by long runners called stolons. The purple, white or deep rose flowers are usually less than 1 in (2.5 cm) across with a delicate scent. hardy to −10°F (−23°C). Johnny-jump-up (*V. tricolor*) grows 12 in (30 cm) tall with ½-in (12-mm) tricolored purple, yellow, and white flowers from spring through early summer on thin, sprawling stems. It is short-lived but readily reseeds and grows in both full sun and light shade. Hardy to −30°F (−34°C).

■ **CULTIVATION AND CARE TIPS.** Most types grow well in light shade, except as noted. Average to humus-rich, moist but well-drained soil is preferred. Set plants 12 in (30 cm) apart.

■ **PROPAGATION.** Seed. Division in spring.

■ **PESTS AND DISEASES.** Slugs; spider mites.

Viola tricolor

INDEX

Page references in italic indicate illustrations and / or captions.

191